JOURNEY

to

SOUL

CENTER

JOURNEY
to
SOUL
CENTER

*Discovering the Gift
of Surrender*

Stacey Brown

SOUL CENTER
BOOKS

ISBN-13: 979-8-9874679-0-9

To my four children, Katelynn, Dylan, Aydan, and Eastyn, my greatest teachers. I will remain fiercely dedicated to giving you a healthier mother today than yesterday. I swear and promise.
Love, Mom/Momma

CONTENTS

INTRODUCTION

When I was in middle school, probably around the age of twelve, we had a class trip where we spent the weekend at a local campground. There, we participated in trust-building activities and group events. The one that stands out to my mind was the trust fall. When it was your turn, you would climb up onto a platform attached to a tree. Facing away from the ground, you would cross your arms over your chest, close your eyes, and then lean back, falling into the arms of your friends gathered below. It was blind faith that the friends would catch you.

It's a concept that I've come to know well over the last several years, as life has taken turns that I never expected. Repeatedly, I'm reminded of the sixth-grade class trip that became symbolic of the trust falls that I would have to do again and again on the journey to my healing. Since the day of the traumatic event that changed my life three years ago, this book has been in me. It needed to be shared in the hopes that it will inspire you, my dear reader, to see the bigger message in the lessons that life throws your way.

My prayer is that you will recognize that even when it feels like God is not with you, He is, always. And He sends us angels in all different ways to help, even in our darkest hour. I hope that you will enjoy the journey of walking through this painful season with me, where so many lessons have come to my understanding. I have finally seen the light at the end of the tunnel.

1

GOOD LITTLE MORMON GIRL

I can't remember a time in my life when there weren't expectations. Being raised in a devoutly religious home, my life felt consumed by clear-cut rules of behavior and performance. The expectation wasn't based on my value as a person; my value was based on how I performed. Everything I did either made me a good girl, or not.

My father, as a young boy, was introduced to the Mormon faith, or a Latter-day Saints faith, through his parents. The church was known for its charitable stance— helping people who were struggling. From a very early age, my father was aware that not only did his family benefit greatly from donations, but the church provided help in various ways when his parents failed to bring in enough money for their basic needs. It seemed the likely choice for him to choose for his own family, offering both structure and a way of running our household that he felt would prepare us for success. Growing up, it was a space with no room for self-love because you were constantly chasing

God's love. And you were chasing His love based off how you behaved, the things that you did. The mentality was that a life of sacrifice was worth it if it meant that you had a ticket into heaven. Mormon culture is one of men being the leader of the home, and the wife is expected to be submissive to that man and his God-given priesthood-holding power.

It's hard to say what of my upbringing was Mormon culture and what was my family's personal interpretation of the Mormon faith, because the lines were so blurred between the two. And though Mormonism is just one example of a religion that forces us into a role or a way of being, it was the practice that I knew, and it was conveyed to me every day, that it was the only right way to live. I remember even as a very young child, knowing that there was an expectation of me, and that my role as a daughter was that I was expected to be obedient. The rules were rigid and anxiety-filled and I constantly felt like I was falling short.

The Mormon faith has a structure of rules one must follow in order to be considered a worthy, upstanding member of the church. As a teenager I was expected to attend early morning seminary Bible study five days a week before my regular school day started. I had to maintain an 80 percent attendance rate in order to complete the program. In addition, Mormon adolescents were expected to attend youth activities one night per week. And church on Sundays was a three-hour event the entire family had to attend.

Dating was strictly prohibited until the age of sixteen, and even then it was only allowed to happen in groups. Youth were required to meet with the bishop of the congregation one to two times per year to be interviewed and questioned about how we lived our lives—to ensure we were following the rules of the church. Topics included monthly tithing, intimate details of our interactions with the opposite sex, inquiries about possible promiscuity, and consumption of forbidden caffeine, alcohol, and drugs. The process was uncomfortable and intimidating. Every day felt like it started and ended with a long list of expectations I was never able to fully meet. The pressure was soul crushing.

My relationship with both my parents was complex. My father was a devout priesthood-holding male, who held various roles within the church, including being a bishop at one point. Similar to a priest, he was called upon to care for his congregation and mentor and advise people in their marriages, family dynamics, and personal struggles. It was a role that he took very seriously, and many turned to him for advice and for his wisdom.

But behind closed doors, his role was very different. He was forceful. He was powerful. He was intimidating. My father spent so many years working his way out of the poverty that he grew up in that he cultivated a single-minded focus on success. His reputation meant more to him than anything else. It was not uncommon to go to church on a Sunday and have someone approach me from the congregation, telling me how lucky I was to have a father who was so devout, so kind and loving. But the father that *I* knew was one who very often used guilt, shame, and intimidation in the raising of me and my sisters.

My mother, a quiet soul, was passive. She was a stay-at-home wife and regularly submitted to the opinions of my father and his way of doing things. Her way of being a loving wife was to always allow my father to take the lead in how the house was run and how we were parented as young girls, even while he traveled regularly building his career. He was so intent on making a future for us that was better than what he had experienced. The drive to be something more consumed him. My mother would follow along with whatever plan it was that my father had, whether it was moving us to a different location or accepting another job. She would pack up the house and move into the next season with him, always doing what he asked.

I'm the oldest of three girls. My sisters and I were never close as young kids. It's interesting because when I look back on it, I recognize now that we were each trying to save ourselves. If you knew that there was going to be a problem with my father, there was a dynamic that happened in the house almost instantly. Being the oldest of the three, I was the one to receive the anger, the guilt, the shame, and the abuse. My second sister, Stephanie, would go into her room and hide while my father yelled. And my youngest sister, Erin, being a quiet soul like my mother, would find refuge under her own bed.

You would think that the common plight of three girls would unite and become even closer in their bond because of what we were facing in our home, but instead it caused a split. Our father made sure that we knew that we would be in even more trouble if we stood up for one another. And so very early on we were divided between loving each other and saving ourselves.

I knew that my house ran differently from my friends. When I would go over to a friend's house to spend a weekend afternoon with them, the dynamic in their home seemed to be so much more relaxed and accepting than where I was living. It was hard to find refuge in any of these homes because the time that I was allowed to do the things I wanted to do was so limited. But I'll never forget my friend Jim. We lived a street apart, near a large highway, but it was within walking distance. Jim was a lover of all things Disney. He was a writer. He would send me little notes at school and leave them in my locker, encouraging me, supporting me. I guess at that point you could call it puppy love.

But for me, Jim became a safe place to land when the regimen of abuse and heartache was too much to bear. I often remember putting on my running shoes and navigating the street with eyes filled with tears, anticipating the hug that I would receive from him in support. I needed someone in the world to know what I was facing, and yet I was afraid to speak it to anyone else. Jim became a best friend, a safety net when things became too challenging.

Around the age of thirteen, I started to struggle deeply with my mental health. Anxiety was something I faced every single day. Whether it was packing up my bag and waiting for the bus, taking a big test, or writing a report, everything had the energy of anxiety, anticipation of what was next, and worry that I wasn't enough. Anxiety made way for depression. In middle school I felt like I was in a world where I didn't fit. I was one of the only Mormons in my school, so the idea of having another kid who understood how I felt was not an option. It was me in a lonely sea of confusion, riddled with guilt and shame.

My mother loved watching her soap operas every day before we came home from school. But her favorite thing was watching *The Oprah Winfrey Show*. I remember on one particular day, coming home from school and sitting by her side while she was watching an episode of Oprah's show. Marianne Williamson was on the episode talking about the difference between religion and spirituality. She was talking about the foundation of everything in this life being either one of two things: fear or love.

She didn't talk about the regimented ways that I was raised. She was simply talking about the energy of the space that we cultivate, and that when we operate from the space of love, we not only heal ourselves, but we have the power to heal others. And collectively we can raise the vibration of the planet. I had never heard conversation like this before, and yet I felt a deep knowing within my soul that there was something this woman knew that had not been shared with me through my traditional religious upbringing.

I went to the mall a couple of days later with a few friends and entered a bookstore where I found *A Return to Love* by Marianne Williamson. I brought the book home, grabbed a highlighter, and went through the chapters, pouring over her words, understanding a greater vision of the universe and the way souls exist on this planet in a manner that had never been described to me before.

It was a taste of a new and loving way of being. And yet I was living in a life that, for a young child, felt like hell.

Around this time, my anxiety and depression were ruling. I don't recall what I had done to get in trouble with my father, but I remember thinking I don't want to do this anymore. I grabbed a bottle of Tylenol, the only medication I could find in the house, and proceeded to pour the pills down my throat. I didn't want to live this way.

My parents discovered that I had taken the bottle of pills and they panicked. I remember my father asking, "What is wrong with you?" They actively pursued getting me mental health help. And a couple of nights later, I lay in my bed, staring at the ceiling, asking God, *Why?* It was the first time where I remember having a profound spiritual experience. I felt what I believe was God cocooning me in my bed. It felt like a warmth that spread from head to toe. It enveloped me, and I heard the words, *Hold on; there's more.* That voice was such a quiet one. It was my inner voice, my intuition. My soul was reminding me, encouraging me, supporting me, letting me know that there was so much more to life than the way I was being raised. And though I didn't understand it then, I look back on it now, and I recognize that my intuition was stronger than my upbringing. I continued to hold on, gripping tightly to Marianne Williamson, to her words, knowing that when we let our light shine, we give permission for others to do the same.

And I wanted my light to shine; I wanted to be a bright spot in other people's lives. I wanted to find my way even if it wasn't clear yet.

I knew that there had to be more.

LIFE LESSON: Our parents raise us based on their experience and upbringing—not always in awareness of what's best for us. When we come into awareness, we realize that we get to choose: Does our program define us? Or do we define ourselves?

QUESTION: What defines you? Your upbringing or you?

2

MARRIAGE AND ESCAPE

Growing up, it wasn't uncommon to go to the church and attend social gatherings. The church held dances for the kids, starting at ages twelve and thirteen. Though we weren't allowed to date until the age of sixteen, we were allowed to have social gatherings like dances under the watchful eye of the youth leaders. Although I had recently broken my ankle, I still wanted to go to the church dance that was being held one weekend. I was not going to let a cast and crutches stop me from being social with friends who I got to see very infrequently.

Walking into a church dance was always so exciting because it was one of the few times that we were allowed to have some fun. At this particular dance, there was a six foot four, good-looking older boy who caught my attention.

Ken was the epitome of the handsome, outgoing, fun guy who drew in lots of attention from the girls. I was four years younger than he was, and yet somehow he found the girl who came wobbling down the hall on her crutches, braces on her big smile, appealing. I came home from that dance completely enamored with this boy. I mentioned his name to my parents and my dad was filled with confusion, stress, and concern. Because my dad was the bishop of our congregation at church, he was familiar with the boy's family and a lot of the problems that they faced.

He warned me over and over again that this was not the boy for me, and I was not allowed to date at such a young age. And like a typical teenage girl, I didn't want to listen. I was crazy about this older boy and the attention that I received from him. Over the next year, we spent every day on the phone and writing notes to each other that we would pass back and forth during our early morning Bible study. It was the closest thing to a relationship I could possibly experience at that age and I was completely consumed with anything and everything about Ken.

With my father constantly pursuing his next career move, my family moved frequently. And so we bid farewell to New Jersey and moved to North Carolina to start the next phase of our lives. Ken decided to go on a mission for the Mormon Church. During this time, we lost touch. Unbeknownst to this heartbroken teenage girl, he had been writing me letters for the last several years that my parents intercepted and threw away, trying to keep us from communicating with each other.

I turned my focus inward.

As my senior year was coming to a close, I was excited to have the entire summer ahead to make memories with my friends. Unfortunately that excitement was short lived. My father received a job offer that would relocate us once again. Soon after the school year ended, we packed up and moved to Maryland.

When I graduated high school, I knew that I wanted more. I always had this deep desire to be a hairdresser. On one occasion, I finally found the courage to bring it up to my father. I really believed that I could make my way in the beauty industry.

He adamantly told me that was an unacceptable career pursuit and that I would not be blue-collar. My grades weren't quite good enough to get into Brigham Young University, the sought after Mormon college in Utah. And so we settled on the decision of heading to Ricks College in Rexburg, Idaho, now known as BYU-Idaho. My parents packed up the car one weekend and we headed to the airport to go and visit the college in the middle of nowhere. How on earth was I going to make a life in the middle of nowhere? I knew that the decision to go to this college was not mine, and yet I felt like I had no ability to speak my truth.

And so, regrettably, I packed my bags and headed off to school to a place where the rules were almost as strict as they were at home. Men and women kept in separate dorms. There were curfews to follow and standards to live by.

But I hadn't gotten over Ken. As soon as I got to the campus, I started seeking out answers to find him. By some beautiful stroke of luck, he happened to be on the same campus at the same college in the same town in the middle of nowhere. I found where he was living, went to his dorm, and knocked on the door. I'll never forget the moment the door opened and his face lit up because the little girl with braces on her teeth hobbling down the hallway on crutches was now a young woman ready to pursue a future with him.

From that day forward, we were inseparable. We built incredible memories with friends in the town in the middle of nowhere. We laughed, we grew, we were in love. Only a couple of months later, we were engaged. I called my parents to share the news with them and I was met with disbelief and anger. My father was beside himself with my decision to marry the forbidden guy that he had warned me about so many times before. What ensued was a battle between two young adults deeply in love and two parents losing control. After a very intense discussion with the dean of the school, we made the decision to leave the college and head to Utah to be with some of Ken's family. Our goal was to be together no matter how hard the path was and we weren't about to let my dad's anger stop us.

In Utah we started searching for jobs and living together. We were surrounded by other young Mormon couples who were newlyweds and starting out their lives. They embraced us, which made it easier to forget about the scrutiny we were receiving from my parents. Nevertheless it became evident that our choices were shaming my father and who he felt he was in the community. He learned where we were staying and called me one day on the phone to let me know how disappointed he was by the decision I had made to leave school, and even more so, in my decision to share my life with a man who he felt was a danger to me.

"Stacey, you have three weeks to come home, plan your wedding, and then get out," he said. "You've made the decision that you want to move forward with this relationship and we don't support it."

In that one conversation I knew that I had shamed my parents more than I ever had before. I dreaded returning home and facing them. While I was planning my wedding in a few short weeks, I was reminded daily and often how disappointed they were in me. What should have been a joyful time was riddled with all-too-familiar shame and guilt. I couldn't escape fast enough.

I got married two months to the day after my eighteenth birthday. In hindsight, what the hell do you know at eighteen? I had never held a job. I had never paid a bill. I had no marketable skill. And yet I was convinced that I was ready to be someone's wife. Ken and I had a small civil ceremony in my parents' home attended by only a few close friends and relatives. Between my parents being greatly disappointed that their daughter was not getting married in the Mormon temple because she wasn't worthy, the acknowledgment that I was marrying someone that they didn't even want in my life as a boyfriend (let alone a husband), and two families who were so divided standing on either side of the aisle trying to do what they could to support the children who they didn't agree with—the entire energy of that day was sadness.

We packed up our U-Haul and drove from Maryland to Utah to start our life together. It didn't take long before the enjoyment and excitement of being newlyweds turned into a marriage with issues. Imagine a young guy with a big ego trying to be a husband and a young girl with no life experience trying to be a wife. Within a couple of years, we were pregnant with our first child, Katelynn. The pregnancy was riddled with significant health issues, including an appendectomy at seven months pregnant. The incision got infected. An illness riddled my body. By the time Katelynn was born, my health had suffered greatly and depression started to rear its ugly head again. The fluctuation of hormones after having a new baby and being twenty years old, plus the weight of the decisions that we had made, became too much to bear as I tried to navigate getting my health back and being a new mom.

I made the decision to move back to Maryland, and Ken begrudgingly supported the decision. We moved into an apartment that my parents had in the basement of their house. My father always had a hero complex. He would be disappointed by his daughters' actions and then swoop in to "fix" things. I believe my mother played a huge part in this. She loved the idea of being close to her first grandchild. I hoped things would be better between us now that I was navigating adulthood.

The issues between Ken and I continued to grow as we faced sleepless nights and the new world of parenting. Our fights became more volatile. I was desperate to feel whole, to feel safe. And when I couldn't feel that way with my husband, I plummeted into self-medication and self-destruction. I remember one particular day after a fight with Ken that had left marks on my body, I approached my father and pulled up my sleeve to show him the markings and let him know the severity of the volatility of our relationship.

My father looked me in the eyes and said, "You've made your bed, now lie in it."

I was trying so hard to speak my truth, to use my voice, and I wasn't being heard. Instead my father chose to call an emergency meeting between my husband, my mother, and me. My father brought a yellow lined legal pad containing a long list of all the ways that I had failed not only both my parents, but my husband. There was no reprimand or accountability assigned to Ken. Some of this could have been due to the patriarchal hierarchy of our Mormon faith. Everything was always my fault in my parents' eyes.

The guilt, the shame, and the humiliation were overwhelming. The only thing that I knew to do was to continue to take it out on myself. I had little to no exposure to alcohol before this time. But I started spending time with different people I'd met through work and school. I would wait for Ken to return from work and then quickly change my clothes and head out for an evening at a local bar or club. I sought out opportunities to temporarily escape the pain and heartache through alcohol and late nights partying.

Sometimes the struggle became so great that I would use alcohol to take myself to a point of blacking out, not remembering the events of the night before. I had no gauge of what was normal when it came to the use of alcohol and other substances, because none of those things existed in my house growing up. But I knew that when I was drinking, it numbed the pain of a situation where I felt like I had no control. I was constantly aiming to escape my reality, desperately wanting it to be something different. I was trying to be a new mom. I was trying to go to college. I was trying to build a way to move forward from what my parents had raised me in. And yet the weight of the expectations placed on me felt so overwhelming, I was unable to carry it.

My marriage ended a few months later and I started navigating the world of being a single parent. Ken moved a couple of towns away to be closer to a woman he had begun sharing a new relationship with. I tried to find my new normal with a co-parenting agreement and visits with Katelynn that Ken limited to every other weekend. I continued to live with my parents, though my father was around less and less. He was on the path to pursuing yet another job across the country, so my mom and I stayed in Maryland while my father traveled to Omaha on a regular basis.

I never remember seeing my parents have more than a small argument. There was never a time when I questioned whether their marriage was healthy or intact. Yes, my opinionated dad was the one who made the decisions, but my mom made the choice to be passive in those decisions, which made me feel like their relationship was forever.

But it wasn't.

Through a series of overwhelmingly painful events and circumstances, my father abruptly and publicly left my mother. And at the same time, he made the drastic decision to both leave and denounce the Mormon Church to pursue a completely different way of life. For twenty-two years, I had been taught that the Mormon faith was the *only* true way to navigate this life. And now, all of a sudden, the man who had been so strict and regimented in his beliefs and his values had completely turned? It felt like my life was a snow globe that had been turned upside down and shaken fiercely, and then set back down to watch everything settle.

My mom went into a deep and dark depression. My sister Erin was battling her own mental health issues. And the man I thought that I knew so well was gone, and my world was turned inside out. And yet I felt like it was expected that I "keep going." I had to be the strong one while my family was crumbling.

I continued to pursue college part-time while working a job at a local dental office. And during that tumultuous time, I met and fell in love with Mark. Unlike Ken, Mark was soft spoken and gentle. I loved the chemistry that we had when we were together. There was something entertaining about trying to pull this introverted person into a conversation. We enjoyed taking Katelynn to the beach. We delighted in dinners out. We constantly had adventures together. Pretty soon, we were pregnant with our son, Dylan.

Once I got pregnant, we made the decision to get married. I was still looking at marriage as an escape. I desperately wanted to create my own family unit and define it differently from what my parents had shown me.

When Dylan was born, unbeknownst to us, he aspirated fluid into his lungs. He was the biggest and sickest baby in the NICU. He spent two weeks intubated with a chest tube, having machines do the breathing for him. There's nothing like leaving the hospital without your baby. I spent every day waking up to a breast pump, letting me know that it was time to feed my absent baby, pumping the milk and then driving to the hospital to deliver it to the nursing staff. Mark and I bonded closer than ever—the only upshot to the challenges we faced. And yet once again, postpartum depression riddled my mind, body, and spirit.

I became consumed with fearful thoughts about Dylan's sleeping, his eating. Bringing him home felt like one of the scariest things I'd ever done. Once I recognized how unstable I was, I sought the help of a psychiatrist who heavily medicated me, hoping to get some relief from the intrusive thoughts and depression. I found little to no comfort. Shortly after we brought Dylan home began the several-months-long process of me being in and out of various mental hospitals, trying to get control of both the hormonal imbalance and the chemical imbalance going on in my brain that were constantly making me think about suicide. It took three hospital stays and the help of one amazing doctor to finally get me on the correct medications, with a plan for outpatient therapy, before I experienced relief. It's amazing to think that I wasn't happy within myself, and yet I was so deeply in love. I had a partner who was loving and kind, an amazing father, a wonderful friend, someone with whom I felt the deepest bond, and it continued to fuel the desire to create a home life different from the one that I had before.

So, two years later, after welcoming Dylan into our family, we welcomed a second son, Aydan. We were so excited about the idea of expanding our family and had finally found some stability. We had three kids and I was now a stay-at-home mom, spending my days changing diapers, making snacks, and scrubbing toilets. All the things that I had said that I wanted in my life were happening. And I was with a partner who was supportive. Away from the Mormon upbringing that I had spent so many years struggling with, now it was about my family. It was about *my* journey.

Again, because I didn't grow up in a home that had alcohol—we didn't even have coffee—I had no gauge for what was "normal" when it came to drinking. Mark would occasionally come home in the beginning of our marriage with a six-pack of beer and we would engage in a couple of drinks to unwind after his busy day of work.

I never had cause to worry, because I knew Mark's heart. I had no awareness of addiction, what it looked like, what impact it could have on a family. But as Mark's job continued to grow in responsibility and our financial needs became greater, the six-pack turned into a twelve-pack or an even larger case, and he would spend late nights sitting on the couch with his laptop, steadily drinking one beer after another. His behavior was never violent, never harmful to anyone else, so I continued to try to play along, turning a blind eye to something becoming an increasing problem within our relationship.

His emotional dependence on alcohol became so great that we became distant one with another. I would try to talk to him about his alcohol use and he would hug me and apologize, but soon we would move on and create the same pattern again. The cycle continued over and over. And when I tried to talk to him and I couldn't get anywhere, I developed the mentality of *if you can't beat him, join him*. And so I found myself cracking a beer at night and trying to keep up with the level of alcohol that he could consume. But I realized I couldn't keep up. Somehow his dysfunction played into my own.

Mark and I had navigated through a challenging season with my postpartum and now we were facing his struggles with alcohol addiction. It became clear that the dysfunction had a ripple effect on the entire family. We had three beautiful children, our first home, and we were falling apart.

We were crumbling under the weight of the expectations that we had of ourselves and of each other. I knew at this point that I had to pursue something for myself. Being a stay-at-home mom was not enough for me. I finally made the decision to go and look at a local beauty school. The dream had never gone away of wanting to do hair, of wanting to help people and make them look and feel more beautiful. I quickly registered for classes and excitedly made the decision to begin pursuing my career.

I WAS ONLY six weeks into beauty school when Mark and I made the painful decision to separate.

The day that I drove away from our house with my van packed, filled with my stuff, I remember thinking to myself, *I'm never going to love anyone like this ever again.* I visualized myself closing off a part of my heart that no one would ever have access to because I never wanted to feel this way again. But when I walked into the beauty school, it was like angels were singing. It was the first time where I put my own desire, my own needs for myself into something without the consideration of another person. My creative juices were flowing. I was making connections with other women who loved the beauty industry. I was gaining self-esteem and purpose.

I was pursuing a dream solely for me, without including someone else on the journey. And I was thriving. For the first time I was showing my children the power of their mother and the desire to show up in the world. I made a lot of friends during this time as I navigated being a single mom with three kids while trying to pursue a career. Two of my classmates, who were cousins, expressed that they had an uncle who they thought that I would get along with. And I agreed reluctantly to being set up on a blind date.

I was up in my bedroom getting dressed for the date when I heard a car pull into the drive. Through my bedroom window, I looked down at the little black Acura sitting in my driveway and Will getting out of the car. He was completely not my type. And yet I decided to push through the initial anxiety and go to dinner. We talked effortlessly the entire time. Will was funny, charming, even a little bit nerdy, and I felt safe.

One date led to two and then to a third. Pretty soon we were spending time together any chance we could get. I introduced him to my children and they connected right away. Will had a love for football, which bonded him closer to Dylan. And he constantly did things to show the kids that he was invested not only in me, but in them. As I finished beauty school and began the early stages of my career, he continued to be a support for me.

Open to his feelings, Will expressed his love for me repeatedly. Being with someone who was open with his feelings and a good communicator was foreign to me. It was refreshing to be with someone who allowed me to feel seen and heard. And on one particular day, we decided to have a conversation about our relationship. He wanted to be with me. He wanted to marry me. He wanted a family. He wanted all the things that I had wanted and tried before. Maybe this was it. Maybe this was the answer. And though there was a part of my heart that I had closed off, I somehow believed that because we had such a close friendship, we could navigate this season of creating a family together in a loving space. I ask myself even now, was I really in love with him? Or was I in love with the *idea* of being in love with him? I'm still not sure of the answer, but I knew when I married him, it was another attempt for me to create a life different from the way I had been raised. I was desperate to give my children the family experience that I felt they deserved. And I believed that Will could help me accomplish that.

We had a few beautiful years. We made so many memories. Will was blessed with a family that was constantly supportive of him and therefore they were supportive of me. They welcomed me into their family and we spent many weekends having dinner all together around their small kitchen table. Holidays became more enjoyable because we were welcomed as part of a larger, connected family. They loved my children as if they were their own. It felt like I had finally come home.

Even though life was busy with three children, I felt like my family wasn't complete. There was a piece that was still missing—a little girl waiting to be a part of our family. Will had never previously been married and had no children and I had always wanted a fourth child. We decided to start trying a couple years after we got married. After a failed attempt ended in miscarriage, we welcomed our little girl, Eastyn. I finally felt like my family was complete.

When I think about our relationship, I know that Will and I were meant to come together to bring Eastyn into the world. But I had no idea that our marriage would bring struggle to my life again. We didn't argue a lot, but there were issues between us that we couldn't seem to solve. He had battled addiction quietly in the past, but until we were married, I was unaware of the magnitude of his past demons. Between my previous experiences with other addicts, and the added stress of raising a blended family, it felt like we were fighting a losing battle. We tried marriage counseling. We tried talking, and then we decided to divorce. Here I was a three-time-divorced woman with four children from three different men, feeling like a failure.

My career in the beauty industry was thriving and yet my personal life felt like a dumpster fire. And the common denominator was me. Instead of looking at the situation and trying to gain clarity, I turned it inward, blaming myself for failing. What could I have done differently? What was wrong with me that I couldn't successfully navigate a relationship? And now I had these young children who needed their mother and a family, but I felt like I haven't even found myself.

Leaving Will was one of the hardest decisions I've ever had to make. In many ways he was emotional security. He stepped into the role of father with my older kids when Mark was unable to be present due to his addiction. His family became my family, providing me love and acceptance I had never received from my own family. I wanted to believe in the fairy tale, yet it was clearly falling apart. I felt like I had exhausted all the other options. Shortly before I moved out, I sat in our bed, wondering how we got to this place, quietly listening for any messages that might come through. And the same way that I felt God cocooned me as a young teenager, came back to me in a different space in life all these years later. While I sat facing the end of another marriage, I heard God say, *There's more.*

I hoped so, putting my faith in His reassurance.

LIFE LESSON: Changing circumstances does not necessarily change our programming. Unless we face our demons and heal, nothing will change.

QUESTION: What programming do you have based on your circumstances that needs to be released?

3

AYDAN'S ACCIDENT

W hen it came time for me to make the decision to move out from my marital home with Will, I had to tell Mark what was happening because of the impact I knew it would have on the kids and our living situation. It took a long time to get to a place where Mark and I were able to co-parent our children together. But we had established a close friendship over the years as we continued to raise our boys. He offered his support and his encouragement, and we began talking on a fairly regular basis. Mark was familiar with the postpartum depression that I had struggled with after both Katelynn and Dylan's birth, and he saw the familiar signs return with Eastyn's arrival. It was only natural that I would reach out to someone who understood the previous struggles I had been through to help me understand the current struggles I was experiencing.

I've faced a lot of different challenges in my life that required a process of forgiveness, but none that run as deep as the connection between Mark and me. We shared a past where we had both harmed each other greatly. And yet, somehow, here we were, years after our divorce, and me having married someone else and had another child. We were speaking more than we had ever before. We began to take the kids out on different adventures around town, reconnecting and rekindling, not sure of what was next, but knowing that he was a huge support to me during a time when I felt so alone.

We were heading into the summer months, close to Aydan's tenth birthday. Aydan loved to be out in the neighborhood with his friends, riding bikes and enjoying the beginning of summer. He was running the neighborhood while I was up at the local salon doing hair. It was the day of his fifth-grade graduation, a time of celebration and excitement. I couldn't wait to see my little boy walk across the stage. It was a busy time in the salon as well. Clients were preparing for end-of-the-school-year celebrations and wanted to look their best. I took a break from my hectic day, just long enough to go to the school and watch Aydan cross the stage.

We celebrated with a quick hug and then I headed back to the salon. It was extra crazed because I was the only one working that day. My coworker was away on vacation, which allowed me the ability to run not one but two chairs. So, while one client was sitting in a chair with their color processing, I was at the next chair applying color on another client. It seemed understandable that I wouldn't have the time or ability to answer my phone and yet it kept ringing.

Moments later, Dylan and Katelynn's boyfriend showed up at the salon. They walked in the front door, pale faced, and alerted me that there had been an accident involving Aydan and his bike. I felt my body run cold. Both boys struggled to get out the few words they could. I knew instinctively it was serious. I'm not sure if I even took off my rubber gloves or removed my apron, but I ran out the front door. I jumped into the car with Dylan and Katelynn's boyfriend shaking from head to toe, unaware of exactly what had happened. We sat in fearful silence anticipating what we might see when we arrived on the scene. We pulled up to a busy intersection where there was a large semitruck waiting to make a turn. I remember jumping out of the car, running into the center of the lanes of busy traffic and yelling for people to stop so that we could make our way through.

Arriving at our neighborhood, we came upon the scene of stopped cars and an ambulance. Aydan had been out riding a friend's bike through the neighborhood when he came to a busy intersection and realized that the bike's brakes weren't working. And just like any stubborn little boy, the pleas of his parents to wear a helmet while riding his bike had gone ignored. I had no idea what I was going to find when I stepped out of the car. But as soon as I heard Aydan screaming from the ambulance, I breathed a sigh of relief. He was alive.

"What happened?" I pleaded with the female officer who was standing at the scene of the accident. She informed me that a pickup truck had approached the inter-section at the same time Aydan's bike came down the hill. And so he collided with the front of a truck. We knew that he had at least one broken bone because of the magnitude of the break. He lay in the back of the ambulance unable to walk or move his leg. The sound of his screams was the only thing I could hear. A helicopter was requested to come to the neighborhood and airlift us to the local hospital. He was in need of surgery.

A calmness came over me, overriding the initial shock of seeing my child experience such pain. I must have still looked blank or shell-shocked because the officer who was leading the helicopter trip grabbed me by my shoulders and said, "You can get in the helicopter, but you have to remain calm." My numb body moved forward to the entrance of the helicopter and I climbed aboard while my son lay strapped to a stretcher. You would think the adventure of a helicopter ride would be something that I would remember. But the only thing I recall was landing on the rooftop of the hospital in the busy city, and Aydan quickly being wheeled in for care.

We were brought into an emergency room with a large light over the table where Aydan's shaking frail body was. Doctors and nurses scrambled around the table taking Aydan's clothes off by the force of scissors and removing anything that would obstruct them from viewing his injuries. He had broken his femur in half, the largest and strongest bone in the body.

I waited and waited for the rest of the family to get to the hospital. Once I was allowed in the hospital room, I stood next to Aydan's bed listening to the doctors assess his care. His little face looked up at the doctor, tears streaming down his eyes.

"I have a question," he said.

And the doctor said, "What is it?"

"Can I scream?"

"Yes, you can scream as loud as you need to," the doctor reassured him. "Go ahead and scream."

"Oh my God! Oh my God!" Aydan screamed from the core of his being as he trembled. Tears streamed down my face, too, as I felt so helpless, unable to assuage my child's pain and fear.

I was asked to step out into the hallway while X-rays were taken. And as I looked down the hall to the entrance of the hospital, Mark came walking through the doors. We had agreed I would ride in the helicopter with Aydan and he would meet me by car. He was white as a ghost and shaking. I have no idea how he was able to safely drive to the hospital. I had not stopped shaking since the boys arrived at the salon to inform me of what happened. Mark came up to me trembling, and I grabbed him by the shoulders and looked him in the eyes. "There is no time for you to break down. Mark, we have to be strong for our child." He immediately sucked in his breath and wiped his tears knowing that I was telling him exactly what we needed to do. We both pushed back our emotions and waited for the doctors to let us know what it was they were going to do to help our son.

Once doctors got Aydan to a place where he was somewhat comfortable and still in the bed, they relocated him to a room in the upper level of the hospital to wait overnight for surgery. It took hours before he was comfortable enough to fall asleep. Mark and I sat there helplessly next to our son's bed, waiting. As Aydan's breathing became calmer and rhythmic, we knew that he had finally found rest. We stepped out into the hallway, stopping at two chairs beside a large window overlooking the lights of the city at night.

"Mark, we have to pray," I insisted. "There's no one else who can help us with this, but God." I grabbed Mark's hands, our knees touching as we sat in the chairs. And for the first time ever in our relationship, we bowed our heads in humble pleas to God to help our son, to heal him. It was a level of connection that we had never shared before. My prayers were usually something sacred that I did alone in my quiet time. But in this moment, I felt that the power of the two of us praying together, pleading with God for our son, collectively would make more of an impact.

Tears streaming down our faces, we had one of the most divine moments. It didn't feel like just a connection between Mark and myself. It was the first time there was a connection between Mark, myself, and God. It began to stir something within us that we didn't even know still existed. It was like the years we spent apart had never happened. There was an unspoken churning in both of us, a desire to try again, this time in a different way—this time with God.

LIFE LESSON: We can find God in our darkest moments. We are always being guided and protected in some way. We need to be open to God showing off.

QUESTION: Think of a time when you were in darkness. How did God show up?

4

SECOND CHANCE

At the end of my marriage with Will, I became aware of how much my body was suffering. When I went to a routine doctor's appointment for my annual physical, the number on the scale was higher than it had been when I was nine months pregnant with Eastyn the year before. The doctor handed me the paperwork to bring to the front desk of the office, and I glanced down to see the box checked next to "obesity counseling." With those two words, the reality of my body's neglect became apparent, and I knew that I had to do something to make a change.

I had an inexpensive treadmill gathering dust in the basement, and I decided to clear the clothing off the hanging arm rails, plug it in, and start walking. I would walk from one commercial break of *Dr. Phil* to the next, and soon I was walking a mile. And then two. My walking evolved into an awkward jogging pace, and then into a slow and steady run. There are so many profound life lessons in running. It's not just putting on a pair of shoes and hitting the pavement. As you delve in farther to the journey of becoming a runner, you find that every detail matters. You need the proper shoes, the right stride, the consistent pace, and the commitment to show up on a regular basis to increase your stamina.

But the biggest lesson is, the competition is with yourself and not with anyone else.

Unbeknownst to me, Mark had also started running in order to maintain long-term sobriety. He would wake up in the middle of the night, at times, and go out for a three a.m. run, trying to calm the racing thoughts that he had battled for so many years of his life. As we started to rekindle our connection, we found out that the two of us were already running alone. And so we decided to explore the process of running together. The connection with Mark was getting stronger, and the depth of the forgiveness of the past was evident. We found a joint passion in our daily runs together. We would set a slow and steady rhythmic pace next to one another at a local park, or out on the country roads with endless hills. Without words, we would settle into a comfortable pace, every single day on the road together.

We decided to start attending a local church together, based off some friendships that we had made in the community. Being a hairdresser, you meet all kinds of people in the chair. And one of the people I was blessed to meet was a pastor's wife named Kristen. Kristen told us about her nondenominational Christian church that was in the community. She encouraged us to come and experience the environment as a family. Soon thereafter, Mark and I started regularly attending their church services. And eventually, we were leading small groups—healing groups, encouraging people to strengthen their family connections and enhance their marriages through God. Kristen became an incredible mentor to me.

Once, in my living room, Kristen and I sat talking about some of the pain that I had experienced as a child, the regimented expectations of being Mormon, and the pain that had been inflicted upon me because of this way of life. "You know," she said, "you don't have to feel this way."

"What do you mean?" I asked.

"You don't need to feel the shame and the guilt that has carried you for so many years," she said. "You can form a different relationship with God, a loving relationship with him."

And so I began the journey of self-love. It was a concept that was so foreign to me, because the strict upbringing that I lived in defined you as either good or bad. And this new concept was about me understanding that I was divinely created, and loved exactly as I am today.

Kristen decided to start a small group of women who were also struggling in the self-love journey. I was blessed enough to spend weekly meetings with these women, connecting and understanding who we are through God's eyes, instead of being ruled by the decisions that we had made in our lives in the past. My relationship with God began to develop in an even deeper way than I could have ever expected. And I began to understand that it was more about who I am than what I accomplish.

The church held these beautiful services a couple of times a year, where they would gather together and perform baptisms for people who were willing to accept Christ. Though I had been baptized at the age of eight in the Mormon Church, the idea of rededicating my life to God was something that felt very important to me. I wanted to experience the opportunity of going into a large tub of water and being cleansed of those things that I had done in the past, and recommitting and rededicating myself to a life where I was aligned with purpose and my higher power.

On a gorgeous spring day, we gathered on the grounds of the church for a beautiful outdoor picnic and baptismal service. I was giddy with excitement. I was making the decision to dedicate my life to God. It had seemed like such a trivial thing to decide at eight years old in the Mormon Church. But this time, just around the age of forty, I was full of mindful clarity, more understanding, and more purpose. Kristen's husband, Jim, was the pastor of the church, performing the baptisms. He grabbed my hand as I shakingly walked up the steps into the baptismal font. The water was warm, the sun shining down on me, and Mark stood by and watched while the congregation prayed over me. I grabbed Jim's wrists and allowed him to dunk me under the water, completely immersing me in the tub. And when he pulled me up and out of the water, I felt cleansed, renewed, lighter.

It felt like all the religious programming, the prior indoctrination, were being washed away. And for the first time, I was accepting who I was and who I was divinely created to be. Mark and I sat picnic-style on the grass of the church grounds eating a hamburger and celebrating the experience I just had. I recounted to him the magical feeling of coming out of the water cleansed in a rebirth.

Mark looked at me and said, "I think I want to get baptized too."

"Yes!" I cried. And I didn't hesitate to jump up and run across the grounds to the pastor. "Wait, don't dump the water out of the tub yet. Mark, too, wants to get baptized."

And on that same beautiful sunny day, Mark was the

last soul in the congregation to enter the baptismal font and experience the beauty of his own rebirth. It was clear: we were being given a second chance. We were being given the gift of forgiveness from our creator, forgiving one another, and moving forward in a new life that we created on purpose.

LIFE LESSON: Forgiveness—in all forms—is a critical part of healing. So many of us focus on forgiving others, but do not forgive ourselves.

QUESTION: What do you need to forgive yourself for? What would it look like to let go and forgive another?

5

RUNNING A MARATHON

It became all-consuming to get healthy. As I took up running, I began to feel its positive impact on my body, my mind, and my spirit. I was aligning my life in a way that I never had before, because to keep up with a running routine you have to be disciplined. I allotted time for myself every day, no matter how busy life got. My goal was to successfully run a half-marathon, which is 13.1 miles. Leading up to the race, Mark and I spent months training, excited for the opportunity to run with a large group of people and experience the energy of a race.

The week before the event, Mark went out on a run and injured his foot. I was devastated. How on earth was I going to run my first race without my other half? Every training day was done together. Every time we hit the pavement, it was side by side. And now I was facing my first race potentially alone. A couple days after Mark's injury, I came down with an illness that filled my chest with a dry cough and made it hard to fit in those last couple of practice runs before the race. Nonetheless, I got loaded up on antibiotics, steroids, and an inhaler, crossing my fingers that I might still be able to enter the race.

The day before the half-marathon, I made the decision that I was going to run. I didn't know how I was going to do it alone because there were so many times when Mark and I leaned into each other to complete a task, but I was ready to try. We arrived at the grounds of the race, and I remember the head-to-toe cold sweat of my anxiety. I stood at the starting line surrounded by all the other runners, their adrenaline pumping like mine, and as soon as the buzzer sounded, I started to move my feet.

My pace was slow and methodical, even cautious, because I knew that I had been sick only the week before. But even without the prior week's training, I was determined to see my goal through. Most of the race was run on flat ground until at the halfway point we descended down a large hill. I knew that at the bottom of it, I would have to turn around and loop back up. Going uphill was always the most daunting for me. During training, anytime I faced a hill, Mark would be the one encouraging me. Without him, it was just me and my feet and the music playing in my ears.

I probably moved slower that day than during training for the race, but I didn't stop. One foot in front of the other, I watched the mile markers pass before me. Mile seven, mile eight, mile nine . . . I gripped to the hope that I would be able to reach the finish line. My pace fluctuated, the air in my lungs burning, my body dripping with sweat. And as I came around the corner, I saw the finish line that I had been working so hard to reach. I searched through the cheering crowd and there was Mark waiting excitedly for me with open arms.

As soon as I crossed the finish line, I ran into his arms and wept. I did it. I did it all by myself. I did it. Even to this day, I don't know that there's been another race that felt so powerful, because that one I was running alone.

The beauty of running is its rhythmic pace. As your feet hit the pavement, it's meditative. It gave me time to contemplate things that otherwise didn't get thought about. And it was a time for me to get clarity. It was my time with God. On some days, after the race, there were times when Mark and I couldn't run together and I would take that time to throw my shoes on and go out on our road, running past the houses of our neighbors.

On one particular day, I was deeply struggling with the relationship with my mother. She is a very soft-spoken woman, an introvert by nature. I believe that she loved her children fiercely, but that she didn't love herself. It became challenging to forge a relationship with her because I was constantly looking at other people and the loving, safe relationships that they had with their mothers. I longed for the loving arms of a mother who would comfort me when I was in pain and cheer my successes.

On this day, as I was getting ready for my run, I thought about how angry I was. God had failed me. He had given me a mother who found affection challenging and who rarely saw herself as the beautiful gift that I knew she was. As I started my run out in front of my house, I realized how angry I was with God. I deserved more. And as I started to gain momentum on the road in the open countryside, I heard God say to me, *You're right. I didn't give you the mother that you deserved.* And then he added, *But guess what I did give you?*

He proceeded to show me beautiful mental snapshots of all the women who had come into my life over the years and mothered me. The friend who brought me a meal after having a new baby. The women who showed up and rallied around me when my marriage was ending, and I had endless boxes to pack and move. The number of times when clients of mine would come in with a fresh meal or a coffee. Yes, God had failed giving me the mother that I desired. And yet he had found ways to allow me to be mothered through other women who came into my life at exactly the times that I needed them.

This is the story that I have shared often with clients who struggle with the same thing. It's helped many people to gain clarity on the relationships with their own parents, where we felt like we deserved more, and God has given us more, but maybe we forgot to look at it.

ONCE YOU'VE RUN A RACE, it's like lighting a fire. You're constantly scrambling for the next opportunity to set a new goal, a new personal record to go a little bit farther distance than you did in the race before. Mark and I got brave and signed up for the Baltimore Marathon: 26.2 miles through the biggest city in our state. It was something that was going to take an insane amount of discipline, but we were determined. The day of the race came and we were both so excited as we walked through the throngs of people throughout the city, some running the race, others there to watch and cheer us on.

The excitement was palpable. Mark and I were as prepared as we were going to be. And yet we both felt so insecure. As we made our way through the crowd to the starting lineup, we looked at each other, squeezed hands, and reiterated our game plan. If one of us couldn't keep going, we would leave the other one behind. We were determined to encourage each other to finish the race even if one of us couldn't.

And with a signal, we were off.

The weather that day was beautiful. The sun was shining, spectators lined the streets, and a refreshing breeze blew through the city. It was the perfect day for a run.

We made our way through countless rolling hills, keeping a slow and steady pace, being sure not to leave the other one behind. It was clear how in sync we were after training so many months side by side. I wonder why being in sync out on the open road was so effortless, yet we rarely spoke more than a few words to one another. Mark has always been quiet by nature. We bonded without the need for much communication, which was right up his alley. We would stop for the occasional snack or water along the way at the various stations set up throughout the city. And then we kept on going.

Mile ten, mile eleven, mile twelve . . .

At mile nineteen, my body started to give out, becoming shaky and unstable. It felt like I was trying to run with cement blocks on my feet rather than my expensive running shoes. My run slowed to a jog and then a painful walk. I felt like I couldn't go on anymore. "Mark, I have to stop for a bathroom break." We walked over to a row of porta potties lining the side of the street, and I waited in line, my wobbly legs feeling like they were going to collapse out from under me.

Once inside the bathroom, I sat down and began to cry. I had completed nineteen miles. I had almost made it to the finish line. And now it felt like I was going to have to quit. I was going to have to tell my running partner to continue without me. I pulled my phone out of my running pouch and saw a text message from my friend who was going to meet me at the finish line: *Stacey, I'm here waiting for you. I can't wait to see you.*

I responded: *I'm not going to make it. I can't go anymore. I'm sitting in a porta potty on the side of the road and my body is done.*

She replied: *You'll be here. Doesn't matter how long it takes. I'll be waiting for you when you get here.*

I made my way out of the porta potty and looked at Mark. "I don't know how I'm going to do it, but let's try to keep going," I said.

We began with a walk and then a slow jog. And we kept that steady pace all the way to the last leg of the race.

The finish line came into sight and, on instinct, we reached for each other's hands. As we triumphantly crossed the finish line, we simultaneously threw our arms up in the air. We did it. We did it. It didn't matter that many of the people, both runners and spectators, had already left for the day, that the race grounds were closing, it just mattered that we had finished, and we had done so together.

Running had become a pathway to a deeper relationship with God. It was helping me to become a healthier partner with a deeper connection to Mark. It was teaching me perspectives on my relationships and how I was going to heal.

I was ready.

LIFE LESSON: When you commit to show up for yourself, it has a ripple effect on your life. Creating a space for yourself, and finding a healthy routine, allows you to connect with a higher power and the energy flows into every area of your life. God always finds a way to meet our needs—just maybe not in the way you expect.

QUESTION: What adjustments can you make in your life to make self-care a priority? If you let go of your fear, what goal or dream would you pursue?

6

REIKI AND RELIGION

R unning became such a healing practice for me. It opened me up to self-meditation every day, and a clear understanding of my intuition. This discipline allowed me the space to start exploring other modalities. The question of spirituality versus religion became a question that I wanted an answer for. Where do I fit? The Mormon upbringing that I had been raised in for decades didn't fit, and traditional Christianity, though more comfortable, still left some questions. I became aware that I was connected to something greater, yet I didn't have clarity on how I would show up in the world.

When the kids were little, Mark and I lived in a neighborhood where the houses were close enough together that all the local kids would gather outside, riding their bikes and playing with one another. Our neighbor across the street, Gwynn, was often outside with us. She was eccentric, unique, and a little bit mystical. One day while we stood outside with the kids, I was riddled with a terrible headache. Gwynn shared with me that she had a practice called Reiki, a modality that she had learned and been using in her healing practice for many years. She offered to perform a session on me, saying she felt it could help with my headache.

We left the kids outside with Mark, and I walked into her small home office that contained what looked like a massage table. I climbed atop—game for anything that might help the pain diminish—and as she placed her hands gently on top of my head, I felt a wave of energy through my body. The tension I felt in my head all morning slowly began to dissipate. As she finished the session, I was in awe. I had no idea what I just experienced, but I knew there was some sort of a shift that relieved me of physical pain. I felt a connection to Reiki, but I didn't see myself as a healer.

Several years later, while working behind the chair, I had another friend and client who came and visited me often. She, too, had an eccentric nature about her. Raised in a similar upbringing to mine, where religion was at the forefront of how her family was working, she started to talk about Reiki. Recently she had gone to receive training from a Reiki master not far from her home, and raved about how powerful the experience was. It piqued my interest enough to contact the Reiki master and find out when she would have classes again. I paid several hundred dollars and registered for the next session, excited to see what might be there for me.

I spent an entire weekend in a conference building with other like-minded people desiring to explore a new modality. We learned the different ways that Reiki can impact another. We learned the various skills and hand positions that were needed for this holistic practice and perfected our abilities on each other. At the end of the weekend, I entered into a small room with the Reiki master, where she performed a beautiful ceremonial process to bless me with the gift of Reiki attunement.

I returned home that night excited to try these newly acquired abilities. I knew something profound had happened, but I was curious to see the impact it would have on the people around me. We were encouraged by our Reiki master to take the time to practice self-Reiki, and then explore those practices with our family.

One night as I was getting Eastyn ready for bed, we did our normal routine of brushing teeth and putting on pajamas. Afterward, I asked Eastyn if she wanted to lie on my bed and let Mama do Reiki. She quickly agreed and laid down on a pillow in front of me. I placed my hands gently on her head, just as my neighbor had done for me years before, and I slowly started the process of welcoming in white light into my beautiful little girl's body. Her breathing slowly eased. Her eyes closed, and within a few short minutes she was fast asleep. Mark stood by the bed in awe. He gently picked Eastyn up, carried her to her room, and tucked her in her bed.

Mark quickly came back into our room and looked at me. "Whatever you just did for her, can you do that for me too?" I laughed and asked him to take the same position that Eastyn had on the bed. And then I laid my hands on his head and allowed my life partner, my best friend, the experience of feeling the gift of my healing hands.

As I began to explore Reiki, I began incorporating its tools in my work behind the chair. When I would lay a client back into the shampoo bowl to wash their hair, I consistently welcomed in Reiki energy healing as a way to connect with their soul and provide deeper relaxation and peace during their experience. While performing this, I would often receive intuitive messages of things that my clients were facing in their lives, and internal struggles that they didn't often share with others.

It became a great blessing in my practice, because I was more attuned with both myself and my client. I was able to provide them healing in a way that many didn't understand, but they consistently loved. And it came through in how in demand I was. My business continued to grow as I intermingled holistic practices with my skills as a hairdresser.

I still struggled with religion versus spirituality. I knew that I had been taught that things were supposed to be a certain way. But in the world of healing, it felt like the rules were so much broader. They surpassed time and distance. I was learning that my abilities did not fit within the four walls of a church. They were meant to be shared with the world.

LIFE LESSON: We all have gifts and abilities. It's important to try new things and explore the different ways God can speak to us. Only then will all our gifts and talents be revealed.

QUESTION: If you release your programming, your religion, your upbringing, what healing modalities/gifts could you pursue?

7

SWEET SURRENDER

A s I took the journey toward loving myself, I also started trusting myself, which left me open to exploring different spiritual gifts, like my intuition. After all the years of being behind the chair and working with so many different people in the community, I was very aware that the one thing that everyone has in common is pain. Our pain may look different, but it was clear to me that everyone was walking around with some sort of heaviness on their heart and searching for a way to heal it. I wanted to be a part of their healing process.

I wished to help others on a greater scale than just working behind the chair, doing their hair, and receiving intuitive messages. I wanted to use my voice and intuitive gifts to make an impact. And because of the religious indoctrination I had endured, I felt like maybe the place to do that was in a church or a religious organization. If my gift was from God, then wouldn't it make sense for me to be involved in a church? I approached a couple of leaders in our church, only to be turned away at the idea that I would somehow be able to be in a leadership position.

I felt an intense desire to help other women on their own challenging journeys to accomplish clarity and understand their purpose. So why didn't I fit? My programming from childhood led me to believe that following teachings from a church was supposed to bring me clarity, and yet I felt more confused than ever. Mark and I made the decision together to walk away from that church, thinking that maybe if we tried another church, we would gain more understanding.

Hope Chapel was a small church in a town right near where we lived. We had friends who attended there and spoke wonderful things about this small church and the impact they were having on the community. We began attending Sunday services, and on one of our early visits, they expressed that they had a program coming up called The Discipleship Workshop—six weeks of intensive scripture study and stillness. It was a time for us to turn inward and grow our relationship with God, abstaining from things in the world that might otherwise distract us. We were going to "quiet the noise" for an extended period of time and focus on growing our faith. It was an experience that Mark and I decided to embark on together, and yet it proved to be such an individual journey. We made the commitment to abstain from secular music and TV, and pour all our energy into things that would connect us closer with God.

As a busy mom, any time in the car alone is sacred. I love listening to music and rolling down the windows while enjoying a nice ride. But I decided that I was going to follow the commitment of this discipleship program. And so I pulled up a recent podcast episode that was a recorded sermon from a well-known pastor and his church. In the sermon, the pastor talked about superheroes. So many times we imagine that a superhero is someone with a cape and powerful abilities like flying that are beyond this world.

And then he explained that a true superhero is not someone with superpowers out of this world. It is someone who surrenders their idea of what their life should look like, for whatever God wants it to be. He asked his congregation, "Who wants to be a superhero?" And as I pulled into the grocery store parking lot, I automatically threw my hand up in the air. *I* want to be a superhero. "If you want to be a superhero," he continued, "then I need you to do the following. Put your hands out, palms facing up, and say the words 'I surrender God. Use me.'"

I had no idea that day, as I spoke those words in the car, that I was giving up my idea of what my life would look like for something so much greater than I could ever have imagined. But I knew in that moment, as I sat with my palms facing up, I felt God. I let go of the idea that I needed to be a part of a church, a part of a group, a part of a community, and I accepted that I was on a mission to honor whatever God had ahead for me.

As I WAS EXPLORING ALL these different modalities and ways of being, from church to Reiki to my intuitive messages, I got a random invitation to attend a psychic reading with some of my clients and friends.

It piqued my interest to think that we would all go to one's house and sit in a room and listen to someone deliver us information about our lives that we weren't otherwise privy to. I was curious, a bit nervous, and excited. We arrived at my friend Kammy's house, who was hosting, shortly before seven p.m. to find a woman who I had never met before, standing in the room, oracle cards in hand, ready to deliver us messages. I grabbed some snacks and a cocktail, then parked myself in the corner of the room so I wouldn't be noticed. I wanted to be a spectator. I knew I was meant to be there but I wasn't sure what we were getting into. This was something totally new to me. I was both guarded and curious.

The woman soon commanded the room with her messages, delivering information from deceased relatives who had passed and giving surprising information on events that were happening in our lives. It was crazy. About an hour into the event, she quieted for a moment, and then stood and turned to face me. "You! You have my gift."

Kammy jumped up out of her chair. "I *knew* it," she said.

What? The thing that I had hidden for so long was being called out by someone I had never met, in a space with people who I had spent several years with, working behind the chair in the community. Here I was being acknowledged for my intuitive abilities and it wasn't in a church.

I was being acknowledged for having a gift, and shortly after I was being encouraged to use it. Once the shock wore off, I asked this woman a few questions, trying to gain clarity on what I should do with my gift. What direction should I take? I had tried different churches, different religions. I had explored some new modalities, but now what? She explained how much her life had changed when she started doing readings and using her gifts to help others. She did her best to reassure me that if I was open to it, I, too, would find ways to help others. She was detailed in her readings that day, yet somewhat vague on next steps for me.

But she encouraged me to explore tarot or oracle cards as a way of connecting with my intuitive abilities. I left Kammy's house that night feeling both confused and excited.

I'm lucky enough to live in an area that has a lot of spiritual and energetic history. And one of my favorite places to experience that history is Gettysburg, Pennsylvania. So many battles have been fought there and lives lost. It's a space with a lot of connection to the spiritual world, to the intuitive world. There was a unique woman who owned a place in Gettysburg called The Crystal Wand, a metaphysical shop where you could go to purchase crystals, oracle cards, and other modalities for healing.

I decided to take a road trip to this mystical establishment and see if there was anything that I could connect with. Oracle cards and tarot cards were forbidden in the way I had been raised. They were seen as a form of a crystal ball that was not acceptable. Walking into the store felt taboo, as if I was somewhere I wasn't supposed to be. But the curiosity and excitement overrode any latent fear. Inside the little shop, I was greeted by the smell of incense. Crystals lined the shelves. I strolled its aisles, slowly picking up and examining items, allowing myself to feel the energetic connection.

As I made my way to a back room in the shop, there was a shelf filled with oracle cards. I asked the woman to come and guide me. "I have no idea what I'm doing," I confessed.

"Close your eyes for just a moment," she said. "Now take a deep breath. And when you open them, look at the decks and see what you're drawn to."

I did as she suggested. My fingers scanned the shelf and they stopped at this beautiful blue box, The Avalonian

Oracle Deck. I picked it up and immediately felt like it was mine. "Is this my deck?" I said.

"Do you *feel* like it's your deck?" she asked.

It was like I needed to trust myself in the moment that the deck was mine.

I made a few purchases that day, but the one that was the most powerful was the oracle deck. It was my first deck of cards, the first time I would have the opportunity to shuffle them and feel how they moved. I drove home feeling the conflict between the cards and religion. The Christian community had made it clear to me several times over, that oracle cards and Reiki and the modalities that I was experiencing were things that were not approved of in the religious community. I felt torn between the women that I had grown so close to within the Christian community and the pull to try something more, something new.

I brought the deck home and went to a quiet space in my house to unwrap them. Opening up the box, touching the cards, I began to shuffle them and allowed myself to feel the movement, the energy. Every time I pulled a card for myself, another divine message would come through. It might have been something about my healing, the journey of recovering from the childhood that had riddled me with so much pain. I would gain clarity on how I was showing up in the world. And secretively I began pulling cards every day. It became somewhat of an addiction. Because every time I opened the deck, something new was revealed to me.

If this deck could help me, could it help others? As clients continued to visit me for hair services, I began tip-toeing around talking about my intuitive abilities. I would gauge the reaction of the client and then allow myself to continue more if I felt like they were open to it. Gently letting them know that I now had a deck of oracle cards and I was willing to pull a card for them as long as they didn't tell anyone. Yes, I was that afraid of the opinions of others. I had the confidence that the cards were giving me messages, but I felt the guilt and shame of the opinions of others. As I began pulling cards more frequently, my hands started to move more fluidly and I got more and more comfortable with the idea that I was able to make an impact in a new way. I was learning to trust my intuitive abilities. I was learning to listen to my soul's guidance, and I stopped thinking as much about what other people's opinions were of what I was doing. I started learning how to take care of my own soul and serve others at the same time. I was learning to trust myself, regardless of others' opinions. I was learning to truly show up.

LIFE LESSON: I started to realize that spirituality and religion are two separate things. Taking a leap of faith led me down a path I was not expecting, but gave me exposure to new modalities and ways of connecting with God and angels.

QUESTION: What do you need to surrender that is no longer serving you? What would happen if you surrendered what you thought your life would look like for whatever God/higher power has in store for you?

8

MY FAIRY TALE

As I grew in my spiritual journey, it only strengthened the connection between Mark and me. Our commitment to one another became more powerful, more pivotal. We moved into a small rental townhouse with the four kids and began to create a life again. We had a routine. We spent so much time together, whether we were out running or taking the kids on an adventure to the park. We were truly connected and enjoyed our family reunited.

Mark worked hard to build a career in the IT industry at the same company for seventeen years. But then he learned that he was being laid off. It was a frustrating blow because so many things in our life were moving in such a positive direction. Now we found ourselves with Mark at home with the kids, searching for a job at a time that he never expected to have to rebuild.

Because he was laid off he was given a severance package, which bought us some time and allowed him to seek new employment. We were frustrated, but accepted that this was part of our season. Thankfully, it didn't take too long for him to land a new job. In fact there was still enough severance left over for us to start searching for a larger home of our own.

I was on a mission to find a place that felt perfect for us and our new life. We spent our weekends visiting various different houses that were on the market. All of them fell short.

I decided to start looking on the Internet to see what I might find without the help of our realtor. And probably like any woman trying to build her dream life, I was looking a little bit out of our price range when I stumbled upon a picture of a home that felt perfect.

My realtor sat in my salon chair the next day during her hair appointment and asked if I had seen any houses that I would like her to take us to look at. "Well, there is one," I said.

"Really? What is it? Show it to me."

"Oh, it's a little out of our price range," I added.

"Let's go look at it anyway," she said encouragingly.

That afternoon I followed her car to the beautiful country just on the outskirts of the area that we lived. And as we drove down the street, I saw this beautiful, white colonial sitting in the middle of a field in farm country. As we pulled up to the house in October, the leaves were changing. The landscaping was beautiful. And before I could even exit the car, I heard the message, *You are going to love on a lot of people in this space.*

No one could have convinced me that that wasn't our house after hearing that message. And so I quickly called Mark and told him of my finding.

We had managed to save enough of the severance package to make our dream a reality. It was the beginning of a new season and our family was infused with the hopes of a bright future in our forever home. In this season, it felt like all the sacrifices and hard work were paying off.

At Christmas, Mark put a second ring on my finger. The first time being many years earlier when we had failed. This time the ring was put on my finger with the hopes that our commitment had deepened, forgiveness was granted, and we were releasing the past.

We decided to get married on a Friday in March 2016. A Friday while the kids were already in school. We would rush to the church, have a quick ceremony and then head home to greet them as they got off the bus. That morning I put on my little white dress and Mark donned his gray suit. The air crackled with nervous excitement as we hustled to get ready.

And then the phone rang. Just like anything else in my life, we were thrown a curve ball. Dylan had strep throat and needed to be picked up from school. I can only laugh at this now because the wedding didn't involve any guests, other than the pastor, his wife, and our photographer. We were late to our own wedding.

By the time we got to the church, the craziness of the morning no longer mattered. The pastor and his wife stood at the door to greet us, excited for the journey that they were watching unfold. We stood on the chapel's stage and made our vows that regardless of what we had been through, we were moving forward. We were committed to loving each other endlessly and creating a life with our children again.

As a child I loved Disney movies. In so many of them,

there's the theme of a man swooping in, sweeping the woman off her feet, and her living a life as a princess, happily ever after. On this day, in this church with the pastor, his wife, and the photographer, I felt like I was finally getting *my* fairy tale.

All the pain that I had endured was now worth it because I was experiencing true restoration, healing, and forgiveness. I was finally living my dream, showing up as the person that I knew I was meant to be, and I was doing it alongside my running partner, my forever.

The vows that we spoke that day were so pivotal that I feel I need to share:

"I believe in you, the person you will grow to be, and the couple we are together. With my whole heart, I take you as my husband, acknowledging and accepting your faults and strength as you do mine.

"I promise to be faithful and supportive and to always make our love and our family's love and happiness my priority. I will be yours in plenty and in want, in sickness and in health, in failure and in triumph. I will dream with you, celebrate with you, and walk beside you through whatever our lives may bring. You are my person, my love, and my life, today and forever."

We took so much time and focus on the vows we wanted to say to each other. This time, we were fiercely dedicated to keeping the promises we were making to one another. It felt like the words we were to say needed to be from the deepest place of healing and commitment. Maybe if the words held enough power, we would be strong enough in our bond to never be apart again. We were united and ready for whatever was next . . . or so we thought.

. . .

LIFE LESSON: Too often we feel focused on reaching somewhere, or achieving a goal, when we should really be focused on the moment, its magic, and joy.

QUESTION: Are you waiting on a fairy tale, a happy ending?

9

ANGELS AMONG US

It was clear that I felt like I was being called for more. My life was unfolding in this beautiful fairy tale. I was on a physical, mental, emotional, and spiritual journey that required me to take a closer look at my life. For several years I had been working at a local salon in town and it was just me and the salon owner. Due to things that were happening in her personal life, tension was building. And my unhappiness was increasing. One particularly frustrating day, I made the decision to go to a local equipment supply store and I bought a chair and a shampoo sink and had a friend put them in the back of his truck and drive them to my house.

I had no idea what I was going to do with that equipment, but I put it in the basement and let it sit, hoping that I would be able to do something in the future out of my home. I felt so conflicted being a working mom and trying to juggle my family. Of course, I was no longer doing it alone. Mark was there to support me, but I still felt the pull of being a mother and honoring my career.

During this intense time, Aydan started to develop some health issues. He would randomly get a rash that spread all over his body. It was happening multiple times a month, then multiple times a week, and finally, multiple times a day. He would go to school with the best of intentions and I would get a call from the school nurse at some point saying that Aydan was again covered in the rash and needed to be picked up from school.

For a business owner, this was frustrating. I would cancel my day at the salon, then get into the car to go pick up Aydan, only to have the rash disappear a few hours later. Doctors had no answers and I was worried for my son. I felt more than ever that my presence was needed with my family, but I didn't have a way to move the business home nor the finances to do the renovations it would require. Little did I know that God was about to show off.

Kathy and Dave were friends that we met through our local church. They were a fun couple, and I had connected greatly with Kathy and hoped that Mark would connect with Dave. We had a family trip planned to the beach and at the last minute we decided to invite Kathy and Dave to join us. They agreed to come and we shared an amazing weekend filled with memories, sitting out by the water in deep conversation.

One night we decided to walk the boardwalk together. And while we took in the sights, Dave asked, "Stacey, if you could do anything with your career, what would you do?"

"I know exactly what I would do," I answered. "I would move my business home and create a space in my basement where I could still see clients and take care of them the way I always had. But I would also be present for my family. I feel like moving home and having my business there would create the life that I want in order to be the mother that I need to be to my kids."

Dave began to tell me a story. Many years before, he had the desire to start his own business, but it would have required four thousand dollars to purchase the truck that he needed to be able to get to the jobs with the supplies and tools that were essential for the work that he did. He explained that he had no idea how he was going to come up with that amount of money, when a few short days later, he received a phone call. A local business was planning to remove large filing cabinets from their office space.

If Dave was willing to remove the file cabinets, he was allowed to sell them and keep the money. Dave quickly agreed to this and he sold the filing cabinets for exactly four thousand dollars. He had the money to buy the truck to start his business.

"Stacey, why don't you let me come and see your space?" Dave asked. "Kathy and I would love to see what your idea is."

At the end of the weekend, we returned home and set up a time for Kathy and Dave to come over. I brought them down to the basement. It was not a very welcoming space. The color on the walls was dark. Natural light was at a minimum. And it was littered with boxes of stuff and an old pool table.

But I was undeterred; I had a vision. "Dave, I can imagine it. I'd have a chair right here by the back door. And the shampoo sink would be over here. I can envision the whole thing."

They listened to my ideas and we chatted for the rest of the evening before they returned home. For the first time it felt like my dream of making the basement a sacred space had a little bit of reality to it. Maybe this *was* something I could do. But again, I had no idea how I was going to afford to pay for it.

The next morning, I woke to a text from Dave: *Give me a call when you have time.* I called right away.

"Stacey, God has prompted me to help you create your basement workspace," Dave said. "If you're willing to pay for the supplies, I won't charge you for any of the labor."

I was shocked. Here, in this moment, God was providing me with an earthbound angel who saw my vision for my career and for my family. And he was willing to help make this dream a reality. I bought the supplies—the wood flooring, the paint for the walls—and together with the help of my friends, I cultivated a beautiful, serene, peaceful space within my home, where I could welcome clients and give them the love and care, one to one, that I had wanted to so desperately. And I would be able to do it in a space where I could be accessible to my children at all times.

The beauty of moving the business to my home was it allowed me to create a more sacred space. Clients were no longer coming into a busy salon with hair dryers going and music blaring. Now they walked into my space, my healing space, where they were greeted by me in a peaceful environment that was inspiring their healing.

This also motivated me to expand my Reiki practice. The basement was big enough for me to put a table and a setup to be able to perform Reiki with my clients. I was becoming closer to my family and creating tighter bonds because I was more accessible. And my relationship with my clients deepened because I was able to provide them a sense of intimacy and comfort that I couldn't in the salon.

I was thriving. I was living in a home, in a dream space out in the country, the peace of nature surrounding me. I had a sacred space in the basement where I was deeply loving and serving. And I felt like there was more. Mark was always so good about coming down to the basement at the end of the day to greet me and ask how my day was. And after a busy day, while I swept the hair off the floor, I stopped.

"Mark, I love this life that we've built. I love the fact that I can see clients right from our home, but I can't shake this feeling. I feel like I'm meant for more."

"Well," he said, "we're going to figure it out. We always do." The feeling within me was difficult to describe. I felt deeply fulfilled by how I was showing up in the world, but still I sensed a nudge from God.

I knew I was meant for more . . . but what?

LIFE LESSON: Once you put a call out to the universe, trust magic will happen. Sometimes we need to move out the way and let God show off. Angels show up when we least expect it.

QUESTION: How have angels shown up in your life?

10

BEGINNING OF DARKNESS

It's a beautiful thing when your life starts to look the way you think it's supposed to, when you can feel aligned in how you're showing up and serving others. My personal life was in a beautiful space with my home in the country and my marriage, but there is no time line for our children in the beginning of their struggles. And it became apparent shortly after getting married, that the energy in our home was shifting.

Katelynn made the big decision to move out of the family home to establish her independence and her career as a cosmetologist. I couldn't be prouder of the woman that I saw her becoming. And yet I knew that her absence from the home would have an impact on all of us.

Both of the boys, Dylan and Aydan, were now in high school. It became a priority to them to be accepted and to fit in with their friends. With each choice they made, it was about what looked cool and what the other kids were doing. We began to see the signs of experimenting with substances with both of our boys. It didn't look like a massive struggle at this point. It felt more like an irritation, a frustration, that I had finally accomplished the things I wanted to, and now my boys were both struggling.

Secrecy became a theme in our home. I was being secretive about my gifts and abilities, and who and how I was sharing them. My boys hid their reckless behavior. And now Mark and I were shrouded in the secrecy of the struggles that our children were facing.

During this time, Dylan met his first love, a girl I'll call Zoe. She and her family lived in a very prominent neighborhood in our community in a big home. It was very clear that they had a more lavish lifestyle than what Dylan was accustomed to in our home. He was attracted to the designer clothing and the nice cars.

Zoe's mom struggled with her own children. She was newly divorced and wanted acceptance from her kids, and it was clear in the way she enabled them. She began treating Dylan like one of her own, and he gravitated to her and her home's lifestyle that we didn't agree with.

Dylan got a job working at a local golf course. We thought it would be a great experience for him to wait tables in the restaurant there, making his own money and building his strength in working independently and paying his own bills. Unbeknownst to us, there were people he worked with that made sure he had alcohol accessible to him at any time. It was only after the fact that he confessed to the many nights of getting behind the wheel and driving home at the tender age of seventeen, intoxicated. He was introduced to a fast life of drugs, alcohol, and the excitement of doing things that were compromising everyone in our house.

Here's an interesting thing about trauma, about experiences that you've gone through in the past. There were so many moments watching my young son struggle with patterns that I had already witnessed my husband struggle with in the years prior. It felt like I was reliving a part of my life that I never wanted to revisit. I felt fiercely protective of the home that I had built with Mark, and all the tireless years that went into cultivating healing and forgiveness.

When I saw these dysfunctional patterns with Mark, the first time we were married, I chose to remove myself from his life and from the circumstances that I had no control over. And here I was, years later, watching my son battling the same sort of demons, helpless, unable to control the outcome, and walking away from my son was simply not an option.

My experience with kids experimenting with drugs and alcohol was limited. My sheltered childhood didn't leave any comparison. I felt like I was aimlessly trying to get through each day, unaware of how complex and dysfunctional our entire family unit was becoming. The beautiful early days became a distant memory as Mark and I each coped with our children's struggles differently. I played the role of "fixer," trying to hold the family together and attempting to control what was happening. Mark retreated into his shell, emotionally removed from the gravity of the issues we began to face as parents.

The role of raising teenagers who are struggling in the world was beginning to take its toll. I remembered, years ago, struggling with the same demons with Mark and desperately searching for a way to cope. I was introduced to a beautiful program for families struggling with addicts called Al-Anon.

At one Al-Anon meeting, I listened to a woman speak about the dysfunction that happens in a house where people are using. She said when there is member of the family struggling with addiction, the whole family plays a role in the dysfunction. One person's struggle has a ripple effect, causing the family unit to shift into unhealthy patterns and ways of coping.

It felt like we were all playing a role like puppets on a string, trying to figure out how we were going to face such challenging experiences with our children and continue to maintain the level of healing that we had worked so hard for. Even though Mark and I had been so aligned, we were compromised. We were scared. We were watching the things that we had already dealt with in the past resurface through our own children. We were lost, frustrated, and losing hope.

And it was just the start of our family's troubles.

LIFE LESSON: Even when we as parents feel aligned, our kids go through their own darkness, which impacts us as well. Whatever they are going through, they take us on a journey with them eventually. We can do all the right things, but it does not guarantee our kids' protection. Sometimes we ignore the truth because it's difficult to face.

QUESTION: Are there areas of your life where you are ignoring the truth? Are the challenges yours or someone else's?

11

THE OVERDOSE

Over the years I've been blessed with loyal clients. Some even became close friends. Angela and Kyu were an amazing couple with strong values who embraced me during my years of being a single mom. They would often help me out on days when I didn't have childcare by taking the boys on various adventures while I worked. They even included us in some of their family vacations. We loved our time with them.

Shortly after Christmas during the year of our sons' struggles, they invited us to join them on a trip to theme park Busch Gardens to look at the holiday lights. I was excited to do something in the spirit of the holiday season with my family, and somehow try to make it look like we were all okay. I knew something wasn't right. The darkness was there. But there was no way to be clear on what it was.

We packed up the car that evening, ready to spend a quality weekend together . . . and were immediately hit with an onstream of traffic. The kids were extremely frustrated before the vacation even began.

I was hoping to create some beautiful moments and memories looking at the holiday lights and enjoying the theme park's food, rides, and attractions, but energetically, it felt like there was a giant crater separating our family and no way to bridge the gap. We chose a hotel where we could get adjoining rooms—Mark, Eastyn, and I in one room; Dylan and Aydan in the next room over. Both boys in typical teenage fashion seemed completely uninterested in connecting with us. My expectation was that the boys would want to be with us because we were introducing them to somewhere new and fun. Instead they wanted to hide in their room. (Later, we found out that they were smoking marijuana and avoiding family time as much as possible.) Our family dynamic was notably—and embarrassingly—different than that of the couple who invited us. I tried to paste on a smile. That weekend was one of the last times I remember being able to pretend that everything was okay.

In the early morning of January 4, 2019, Mark and I were awakened abruptly by the sound of a large thud. It jolted both of us upright. My first thought was that maybe we had an intruder. I was shaking. And then we heard another thud. We jumped out of bed and ran into the hallway. Through the crack at the bottom of Dylan's closed bedroom door, we saw his room light was on. We slowly opened the door to find our son sitting on the bed in his boxer shorts, no sheets or blankets beneath him, just an empty mattress and Dylan. He looked very pale and unfocused.

I felt my heart beating out of my chest. Something was very wrong.

"Dylan, what have you taken?" Mark asked. Dylan muttered some words that didn't make sense. He was hallucinating. He was psychotic. We searched through the bags that were sitting on the floor in his room trying to find any answers to the way that he was responding to us and coming up short. We found out later that he had researched online a process called robo-tripping, where a child can take household substances and can ingest them in an effort to get high. We also learned that Aydan was supposed to take part in the robo-tripping with Dylan, and at the last moment he had gotten scared and retreated to his room to hide.

Mark knelt before Dylan, trying to make eye contact and better gauge what was happening, but our son's eyes were vacant. Dylan was sitting there in physical form, but all other parts of him seemed to be somewhere else. Fear coursed through my body.

"Mark, what do we do?" I asked.

"I'm not really sure," he said.

"I think we have to take him to the hospital. We have no idea what he took, and I'm scared."

Dylan continued to try to resist any assistance from us, as he hallucinated talking to friends that weren't in the room. In this state, he was unable to even locate the bedroom door. The thud we heard earlier was him throwing his body against the wall in an effort to get out of his room. He then proceeded to search through his clothing and other articles in his room, looking for, of all things, a pencil sharper. It was terrifying. My son was there, but he wasn't.

We needed to take Dylan to the hospital, but first we had to somehow find a way to get him dressed and into the car. We made the decision that Mark would take him and I would stay back with the other kids. Again, pretending that everything was okay.

Mark went to our room to get dressed as I knelt before Dylan, my hands trembling, my body riddled with fear. I slowly helped him put on his pants and a shirt while he muttered random things, sometimes yelling. My fear increased as his voice carried. I was terrified of the other children potentially waking up and witnessing this horrific event. I was confused. Mark and I then worked together to carefully steer Dylan downstairs and into the car. Mark proceeded to take the trip to the hospital with Dylan hallucinating and yelling the entire way there.

Numb with worry, there was no way I could return to sleep. Instead I lay in bed, staring at the ceiling, watching the minutes tick away, waiting for an update from Mark. I continued to replay the events of the night, wondering how I didn't see the signs alerting me to the severity of Dylan's drug use.

As the sun began to rise, my alarm went off and I allowed my feet to hit the floor. I had to get the other kids ready for school and I needed to stay calm. The last thing I wanted to do was let them know the state that we had found their brother in earlier, and I still had no update of his condition. My role was to be calm to allow the other children in the house to feel safe and to get them on their way for their day at school. As soon as the bus picked up Aydan and Eastyn, I got into my car and drove to the hospital.

I walked into the busy emergency room and asked for Dylan by name. I was directed to a small room where my son lay in a bed with wires and leads coming off his chest and his arms. He continued to be in a hallucinogenic psychotic state for forty-eight hours. The doctors were helpless to do anything other than watch and wait. Throughout the day we started calling drug and alcohol rehab facilities throughout the country, trying to find one that took our insurance and admitted patients under the age of eighteen. You think when you are about to face a crisis, that the tools will be there for you to find a solution, and yet we were finding that our system is so flawed.

Many of the rehabs were private facilities wanting thousands of dollars per week for your child to be inpatient, which was something we couldn't afford. We had no idea how to find a solution. Mark and I continued to sit bedside with Dylan, waiting for him to come back to us. Finally, as his mind started to clear, I will never forget when he looked at me and said, "This is all your fault." And then he proceeded to list each member of the family and how I had failed them.

"Even Dad says it's your fault," he cruelly added.

I felt a deep connection with my guilt. It was like Dylan knew that I had a sensitive part in my heart that felt I wasn't enough and he stabbed it over and over again. I looked at Mark after hearing these ugly words from Dylan and then excused myself to the bathroom to cry.

After wiping my tears, I came out and headed back to the lobby, Mark following closely behind.

I stopped and turned around. "Mark, what happened?" I said, needing to hear the truth from him.

"Stacey, I'm so sorry," he said. "I was frustrated with you a couple of days ago. And as Dylan and I got in the car to run errands, I looked at him and said, 'Don't ever marry someone like your mom.'"

I was crushed. My own husband had said something to our son that was so hurtful. And maybe there was some truth to it.

≈

THERE IS nothing more painful for a mother than seeing their child in pain. But the idea that *I* contributed to that pain was more than I could bear. I felt a deep violation between Mark and me, a division caused by an angry child in pain. I knew that we needed a plan to get him help, and yet I had nowhere to start. We continued to search for a viable rehab and finally found one that had space to take Dylan in. Once he was discharged from the hospital, we packed him a bag and then dropped him off at the rehab facility, hoping that somehow they would fix him.

WHEN YOUR CHILD ENTERS REHAB, the family is required to come to meetings to work through some of the challenges that the child is facing and try to make a plan for their imminent return home. During one of our family meetings, we were encouraged to come up with a family contract—a set of rules that would help to keep Dylan sober. In that meeting, Dylan was encouraged to stop contact with any of the friends or relationships where he had been using or had been in an environment that would be compromising to him.

We asked him not to see Zoe anymore. It was one of the only ways that we would feel comfortable with him coming back home. He refused. During these meetings a lot was uncovered. It became apparent to us through stories from Dylan that he had been getting high with the football team before every practice and every game. I became enraged at the idea that coaches and school staff were allowing this behavior to go on. I became vigilant in trying to find someone to blame, deciding it was time to use my voice and find a way to fix it. It couldn't be that *our* family unit was broken. It must be a break in our community.

I started speaking out about the things I learned, including that the kids at school had access to drugs and alcohol. I rallied the support of our community, informing them of what was happening within our schools. I went to meetings with board members from the education system, principals, and staff. And finally, I organized a community event with a panel of experts to talk about what was happening with our kids and try to find solutions.

During that event, Dylan sat in the second row, leaning back in his chair with his arms crossed over his chest and a smirk on his face. It was almost like he had attained a level of warped celebrity. I thought now that he was home from rehab and a couple weeks sober that we were safe, that we had fixed him. But he was cocky. I thought the addiction component was over, that we had faced our darkest hour and were moving into a season of healing. Boy, was I wrong.

LIFE LESSON: We are all on our own journey. As parents, we sometimes search for a quick fix that does not exist. As our children get older, the decisions they make can have a long-lasting impact on everyone in the home. And yet we may try to fix it with a metaphorical Band-Aid.

QUESTION: What are you trying to fix or control in your life? Is it yours to fix?

12

A MOTHER ON A MISSION, A SON WHO IS LOST

The Al-Anon program was extremely pivotal for me in the days of my first marriage to Mark. Its support program and lessons taught me how to cope. Now it was coming full circle with my eldest son.

Our time with Dylan being sober was short-lived. Rehab centers manage the treatment of addicts as a quick fix. Issues with insurance companies and approval for treatment become a battle, so the goal is to get the addict in and out of the program like they have some viral infection, and as quickly as possible. Dylan came home from rehab still needing help, but the help was impossible to find. The options were limited for meeting our son's dual diagnosis of mental health needs and substance abuse. I spent hours on the phone trying to find a rehab facility for longer-term care, coming up short every time. I became consumed with the idea that somehow someone had an answer for us. Instead, what I found was that rehabs were like a very expensive Band-Aid. I felt like I was walking around with my son, his arm hanging from a small piece of flesh and blood spurting everywhere. I'm screaming for help and the only thing that anyone has is a fucking Band-Aid. I felt lost and helpless.

Through this tumultuous time, I continued to try to run my business, yet I was riddled with the struggles of what Dylan was facing. Anytime I would get a phone call, even if I was behind the chair, I would pick up the phone in the hopes that there would somehow be an answer waiting for me on the other end. The result? As I was trying to help Dylan, I was watching my business slowly fall apart. If my child had cancer, I believe that everyone in my life would be more compassionate and understanding. But addiction and mental health issues are stigmatized. It seemed like everyone else in the world thought the problem should be over, as I did.

We all wanted life to resume back to normal and it was the farthest thing from it. The past several years of Mark and I building a healthy life for ourselves came to a screeching halt. There were no more long runs through the countryside connecting us, bonding us. There was no self-care, no time for me to pour into my own soul and feel replenished and renewed. I was no longer doing readings for people. My life became about survival. I continued to try to find answers for Dylan and there were none. I became involved in the local addictions community, and I met many other mothers who had battled the same disease with their own child. Some of them had paid the high price of losing their child in this life. I wondered often if that was going to be me.

When Dylan returned home from the first rehab, we encouraged him to sign the contract that the rehab had developed, a list of things that we would mutually agree upon that he would do—or not do—in order to be in our home and around his siblings. Dylan refused to sign the contract, the contract that said he would no longer see the girlfriend who had added so much toxic energy into the mix. He was desperate to fit into that fast life with a girlfriend whom he was totally enamored with. We repeatedly asked him to give up his relationship with Zoe to no avail. We thought if we changed his outside influences, the people who were surrounding him, somehow it would fix things. The signed contract wouldn't change things, but I still have a part of me that holds Zoe and her family responsible.

The only thing we could get Dylan to agree to was that if he was going to spend time with Zoe, she, too, would take part in a drug test before visiting with him. The day Zoe came over to the house to see Dylan for the first time after his release from rehab, her mother chose to escort her to our house. I remember churning over the idea of this woman being in my home. Immediately upon entering the back door of our house, she had an unbelievable sense of arrogance about her. She threw her arms around Dylan and reassured him that he was in a great space and how proud she was of him and the fact that he had completed a brief rehab stay. The way that she interacted with my son felt like she thought she knew him better than I did. It felt like she was playing the role of a mentor and acting as if she was a huge part of the solution rather than the problem.

Zoe was only sixteen at the time and it blew my mind to see the degree of freedom she was allowed in her life. Her mother was determined to be more of a friend than a parent and this mother continued to drive a massive wedge between Mark and I and Dylan. At a certain point, as things began to escalate and we saw patterns happening over and over again, Dylan came to us and said that he had made the decision to move out and that Zoe's mom had invited him to move in. There's an unwritten code from one mother to another that when it comes to the behavior of our kids, we stand firmly in unification, that we, the parents, make the decisions. But with Zoe's mom, I felt like not only could she not see my pain, she was determined to take over as a loving mother for my child.

It left Mark and I feeling like we were trying to hold water with open hands. Nothing of these circumstances was of our choosing and yet Dylan believed with every bit of himself that changing his environment would somehow change things. It's only now when I think back to the patterns of behavior in my life that I realize that I, too, have done the same thing over and over again. I was constantly running from circumstances I didn't want to face, believing that changing my environment would somehow fix things. Ironically, I was seventeen the first time I started that pattern, the exact same age Dylan was facing his pain.

We want so much more for our children than what we had. God, I didn't want him to be forty-five and repeating the same pattern. Dylan decided very quickly to move in with Zoe and her family. He abruptly packed his clothes in trash bags, so that he could start a new life as quickly as possible in a new environment. I was sitting on the couch wrapped in a blanket the day he said goodbye. He loaded up his car quickly, then came into the living room where I was sitting. "I'm getting ready to go, Mom." I stood up and hugged him. I told him that I loved him. He gave me his house key and his cell phone and proceeded to walk out the door. He was no longer the little boy that I could protect by giving him a warning or telling him not to do something. He was now the young man who believed he had all the answers.

In some ways, even today, I still hold Zoe's mom and her family accountable for giving my son an easy way out, a ticket to running from his problems. Dylan thought he could fix things by changing his environment. And at seventeen, you think you know everything and your parents know nothing. And boy, was I familiar with that. As I sat back down on the couch after he walked out the door, I felt like my heart was shattered. I felt like I had lost him. The time that I had spent searching for rehabs, battling insurance companies, talking to doctors and therapists, it all seemed pointless. I was left feeling completely helpless. And a small part of me felt relief. The toxic person in our home had left. And for a short moment, though sad, I felt like I could breathe a little bit.

LIFE LESSON: When a family member is struggling, it has a ripple effect on everyone in the house. We can try to control and help our children, but there are many other influences that impact them. They are growing into a world and trying to fit in.

QUESTION: Are you so focused on someone else that you are missing your own needs? Are you blaming someone else for the circumstances in your life?

13

911

April 18, 2019, began as a normal workday. I had a nail appointment with my good friend Pam first thing in the morning. As soon as I got Eastyn on the bus, I headed up the road for my biweekly nail appointment. The roads leading to and from the salon were in a rural area with spotty cell service, but I never missed a phone call. It was interesting, because I felt very relaxed that morning. I had a friend back at the house, working in my salon space to get me organized. I was trying hard to create some normalcy in my life, now that Dylan wasn't at home, now that my life wasn't consumed every day with finding him treatment.

Pam and I had our typical banter about our day, things that were going on in our lives. She pampered me and I felt relaxed and peaceful. I drove home from the salon, knowing that I had a busy workday, yet feeling focused and ready. I pulled the car into the garage, made my way inside, my friend working hard down in the basement, her little girl in tow. As I came down the basement steps, my phone buzzed. It was a text message from Mark. All it said was: *911*.

Mark and I have never used 911, so I knew right away that something was *very* wrong, and I picked up the phone and called him. I don't even think the phone rang once. "Stacey, Dylan's been in an accident," he answered.

I sat down on the basement steps, my blood running cold. "What do you mean, he's been in an accident?" I asked.

"I don't know exactly what happened, but he's been taken to the hospital," he said, "and they're telling me he injured his knee."

"His knee? Okay, what do we need to do?"

"They told me to get to the hospital right away. I don't understand, but they said that he's at Shock Trauma in Baltimore."

"Okay," I said. "I'm on my way."

I asked my friend for a favor, and without hesitation, she agreed to get in the car and drive me. I called the school on the way in the car, and asked for them to have Aydan ready so that I could pick him up. They already knew I was on my way. It felt like they knew something I didn't. We drove up into the parking lot of the school, only to see several police cars waiting in front of the school. The principal and the police were standing next to Aydan as he waited by the curb, pale and shaking.

I don't even remember Aydan getting in the car, but I remember the police asking if we wanted an escort to the hospital. *Why would we want an escort to the hospital if our son just injured his knee?* "No, we'll be fine," I said, not even thinking about the words coming out of my mouth. I just knew somebody knew more than I did, and I had to get to my son. Aydan sat in the back of the car, barely speaking. The silence was deafening.

We drove into the city, and found a parking garage close to the hospital. I walked into Shock Trauma, the automatic doors opening in front of me. People were everywhere. I knew Mark was there, but I didn't see him, because as soon as I walked in, the surgeon came out through the double doors. "Where is Dylan Brown's mother?" he announced.

"I'm her," I said. He escorted me to a bench in the hallway. I faced him, staring into his eyes as he listed the severity of Dylan's injuries.

"Your son is very seriously hurt," he said. "He has a traumatic brain injury, a blocked carotid artery, a second carotid functioning at 35 percent. He has heart valve damage, partial lung damage, a lacerated liver, a shattered knee, a broken elbow, a broken shin. We've put him on a ventilator. We're going to put him in a medically induced coma. He's going to be in intensive care. He's in critical condition." I could no longer feel the ground under my feet. I didn't know if Mark was already there. Did he know what was happening? I was aware there were other people waiting close by and yet I didn't know how everyone knew what was happening so quickly.

I could hear all the injuries that he was listing, and I remember forcing myself to remember each one, so that I could tell the crowd in the waiting room what was going on. And yet in that moment, as I'm staring into the doctor's eyes in shock, at the gravity of what he's telling me, all I could do is stare at his eyebrows. *Wow, he really needs to trim those.* It was like my mother heart couldn't handle the weight of what I was being told about my son. "Please," I pleaded. "Please save my son."

The doctor grabbed my hand. "I'll do everything I can

to try to save your son, but I need you to know that this is very serious."

I walked into the waiting room filled with people. The faces were familiar, and yet, I couldn't register who was there and who wasn't. "I need to get this out quickly," I said. "Here are all his injuries." I rattled them off, and then found a seat. What they don't tell you when you go into a hospital like that is, it's not really set up for those people who are in pain. The small boxes of rough-like tissue are not strong enough to handle the tears of a mother in so much pain. And you're surrounded in a small space by other people waiting for the news of their own family members. It's a darkness like none I've ever experienced before. It's sitting and waiting, knowing that your child's life is hanging in the balance, and that some of the greatest experts in their field are questioning whether they have the ability to bring your son's life back.

Dylan had been trying to get sober through the use of a Vivitrol injection. It's an injection used as an opioid blocker. Luckily we arrived at the hospital quickly because the doctors were unaware that Dylan had taken the injection. It would have been a disaster if they'd administered to him an opioid while under their care. Due to the opioid blocker in his system and the extent of our son's injuries, the only way the doctors could get his pain under control was to use the anesthetic ketamine, the most powerful drug for pain. There were only two bags of ketamine in the entire hospital, and they went to our son. He was now laying in a hospital bed fighting for his life while his parents and loved ones waited helplessly in the waiting room, praying for a miracle.

· · ·

LIFE LESSON: We can have the best of intention, the best plans for the day to carry out a routine, but unexpected things can happen. You cannot always control what happens to you, but you can choose how you are going to react.

QUESTION: Think of a time when the unexpected happened. How did you react? Would you react differently now?

14

THE CHOICE THAT CHANGED EVERYTHING

We knew Dylan had been in a car accident, but we didn't know the details. As we waited for the doctors to do the work that they so desperately needed to do, we started getting pieces of the story. Eyewitnesses reported that Dylan was driving at a speed of one hundred miles per hour on a winding country road with a speed limit of thirty-five miles per hour. There were rumors that this had been a suicide attempt, but it was impossible for us to know without Dylan awake to tell us.

The gravity of a possible suicide attempt was more than my mother's heart could handle. It became clear, as we put the collected pieces together, that Dylan had a very stressful day that morning. As hinted earlier, when Dylan moved out of our home, he left behind his cell phone because we had said, "If you're going to go out and live on your own, then you have to make your own way." Dylan had borrowed Zoe's cell phone that day so that he could make some calls about various things that he needed to get in order for his life.

What Zoe didn't know was that Dylan had been talking to another girl. I'll call her Amanda. He and Amanda had formed some kind of a bond, and Amanda didn't like carrying the weight of that secret. That morning, she texted Zoe: *I need to talk to you.* Since Dylan had Zoe's phone, he was the one to receive that text message, and he panicked. He had begun to create a life with Zoe and her family, and now, this message from Amanda had the potential to compromise everything.

In that moment of panic, Dylan decided that it was better to escape his pain than to face it. He was supposed to be at work that day, but instead, he got behind the wheel of the car, and found that country road, and decided to end it all. As he sped down the country road, there happened to be an eyewitness. Nick was an off-duty Baltimore city firefighter who was helping his wife with her house cleaning business. He was at a house on that road cleaning windows that day, when he heard Dylan's SUV speed past him. He knew that Dylan was going way too fast, but because of his training, when he heard the distinct crack of the car hitting the tree at one hundred miles per hour, he knew that sound well. He jumped into his Toyota 4Runner, and sped down the road to find Dylan's crushed car and his lifeless body.

When he got to Dylan's body, our son was only breathing one to two times per minute. Nick stabilized his airway, and knew that he had to call for help. But when he pulled out his cell phone, there was no service. He ran up the hill until he had a couple of bars on his cell phone to call for an ambulance. He explained the gravity of what he had witnessed with Dylan, gave the location, and when he ended the call, he turned around to find Dylan's car on fire. By the grace of God, he had a fire extinguisher in the back of his truck. He ran to get it, and extinguished the fire before help came.

I know the pain of feeling like it's so great that you would rather leave this earth than face it. It was a feeling that I had experienced many times. But the idea that my sweet seventeen-year-old boy would rather end his life than face his own pain was something I could not wrap my head around.

That day, it was like Dylan put our entire family in the car with him. Our bodies might not have been ravaged with physical injuries, but they were ravaged by one decision. It impacted all of us on a level that even now, I have a hard time describing. Knowing how small our community was, I knew that word would spread quickly, that rumors would swirl around about what had happened, how it happened, and why. How could a child who had so much going for him feel that he had to end it all?

He was a varsity football player. He was smart and talented. He was kind. He loved fiercely. And in one moment, he felt like his pain was too great to face. It was clear that angels were all around us, that even in the darkest of circumstances, God was showing up. And yet all I could think was that I had passed on the legacy of pain and shame to my child, that in one moment, everything changed for our entire family. And I had no idea how we were going to survive it. Dylan made a choice. He made a choice that day to get in the car. He made a choice to try to end his own life.

And I was aware that our choice as parents was tough love. Our choice was to say, *"If you are going to do these things and you are going to live this way and you are going to move out of our home, that you will have to figure it out on your own."* A deep sense of guilt filled my soul. The feeling that our decision to let him go and live with his girlfriend had caused this ripple effect of decisions that impacted not only Dylan, but our entire family and all those eyewitnesses and people who were involved. Was it Dylan's choice alone or did we contribute to that decision?

Even now, this haunts me.

LIFE LESSON: Sometimes God uses earthbound angels to meet us in our darkest hour, someone divinely placed exactly where you need them in your time of need.

QUESTION: Who are the earthbound angels in your life?

15

AN OUTPOURING OF LOVE

I don't ever remember a conversation about who was going to be Dylan's caregiver. I'm not sure if the role was mine because I was his mom and that's what would be expected of the mother, but my career took a back seat to spending as much time as I could bedside with Dylan. Mark had worked so hard to bring his career to the level that he had, and he carried our insurance benefits, and he carried the bulk of the financial weight in our family, so it only made sense that I would close the doors of my salon and focus on my son and his healing.

My entire adult life, my identity, had been wrapped in my ability to serve the clients in my community. I had spent hours behind the chair, tirelessly giving to those who needed my services. I would work late nights and early mornings, and lots of weekends, but I loved it. I loved the fact that I was able to provide a loving space for people in a time that they needed it and make them look and feel beautiful. My worth was defined by my job. And now, I had a new role as a full-time caregiver for my son.

During this time, we became local celebrities, but not the kind that you want to be. I imagine if you were to accomplish some amazing task and the world knows about it, it's exciting when people approach you out in the world and want to know how you're doing. But when your child has been to the brink of death, under the circumstances that our child had been to the brink of death, the last thing you want is to be stopped out in a public area and asked how your child is doing.

It didn't matter if it was a quick run to the grocery store or the hardware store, we would be stopped in public places and not only asked about how our son was doing, but there would be comments about the devastation. "Wow, I can't believe that he lived through this. This has to be so hard for you. How are you holding up?" The questions might seem innocent, but they're not. You're traveling to the hospital every day watching your son's body get more and more frail, watching him fight through the pain of his injuries and the rehab process. It was gut-wrenching.

Our private life became somewhat of a public arena where people speculated on what brought Dylan to the place that he would want to end his own life. Yes, the questions were challenging, the inquiries sometimes embarrassing or hurtful, but the greatest blessing of living in a small community was the way strangers and close friends rallied around us to make life as easy as possible. Our house was constantly buzzing with help from friends, family, and even strangers. Every week, one of my clients would show up with her husband and a trailer with their tractor and they would cut our grass without us even asking. Meals were delivered at exactly the right time for lunch or for dinner.

Our freezer and pantry were overflowing with food sent

to us—foil-wrapped meals, deliveries of staples and supplies, snacks for us to take to the hospital for when we spent all day bedside. Even our parking for the garage and the hospital was paid for. A couple of the women I had experienced the small church group self-love journey with, rallied around me like sisters. They made sure that we had all that we needed, including a GoFundMe. An image traveled around online of Mark and I standing bedside while Dylan's lifeless body lay in a coma. These women cultivated an explanation of our experience and pleaded for the help from an even larger online community. Donations poured in.

We had been so scared to become a one-income family during this time, not knowing how it would impact us financially in the long term. And again, God was showing up and showing off by allowing us the ability to focus solely on our son and his healing. Even the needs of our other children were being met. Eastyn became like a child to the women who worked at her school. Only in kindergarten at the time, these teachers and the school nurse would love on Eastyn and give her hugs during her school day, reassuring her that she was seen and she was cared for. I would walk out to the mailbox on a regular basis to find the mailbox stuffed with cards and well-wishes from people all across the United States.

Our story miraculously touched so many. The outpouring was beautiful, overwhelming, and needed. The best thing about living in the country is that you have a lot of space to be on your property and experience the peace and serenity that only comes from nature. Although we had all these people surrounding us, the challenge for me was trying to find space where I was allowed to let my emotion out. Even with all the love around us, I felt the need to be stoic, to suck it up, to be strong. How could I break while my son was breaking?

Mark and I are the epitome of opposites. I spent all my time trying to figure out how to save Dylan. Mark was never one to communicate easily, but when times were stressful, he would close himself off even more, becoming impossible to connect with. I found this frustrating in previous life challenges, but the distance between us now felt crater-forming.

One particular day, feeling overwhelmed by all the people in our house serving and loving on us, I had to escape. The only place that felt safe to me was my bedroom closet.

I began retreating regularly to this space, leaving the lights off, sitting in the dark on the floor weeping, pleading to God to save Dylan, allowing myself to feel all the emotions. When I was by his bedside, I had to be strong. When I was with my other children, I had to be strong. The closet became one place where I felt safe to be vulnerable and allow the emotions to surface that were constantly bubbling at the top. Many times, my body would be racked with so much emotion that I found myself longing to pray and completely unable to find the words. I would pick up my phone, search through my music, and there would be Lauren Daigle.

The words of her songs were so profound and they became the words to my prayers that I couldn't speak. One song in particular, called "Rescue," contained the resonating lyric: "You are not hopeless though you have been broken." My closet became the space where I could feel God. I could feel that He hadn't left us. I knew this because of the outpouring of the people surrounding us, but I knew it even more when I would take those quiet moments where it felt like I was breaking and God would cocoon me again in that small closet space and allow me to feel a peace that far surpasses any understanding.

I retreated to that sanctuary often as a place to release my pain, to allow myself to breathe and to grieve. Shortly before Dylan's attempt, a movie was released called *A Star Is Born*. It's a dark story where Bradley Cooper and Lady Gaga have a tumultuous relationship while Bradley fights his own demons. His character riddled with some of the same battles that Dylan was facing. He began to speak so much of Bradley Cooper. He idolized him. And the movie seemed to resonate with him on a level we didn't understand at the time, but we became very used to hearing the soundtrack playing from his room. When your child is lying in a hospital bed fighting for his life, you become a warrior determined to fight any and every battle you can, not caring what the world thinks.

I became consumed with the idea of somehow reaching Dylan through the music of this movie. I sat bedside and sang to him while he was in his coma, tears streaming down my face. Mark was able to capture a video of me singing to Dylan and I made the choice to post the video online. It wasn't rational; it wasn't thought out. It was an impulsive dream to try to reach for Dylan. Maybe if I put myself out there, I could find a way to connect Dylan with his idol, Bradley Cooper. If I was going to lose my son, I wanted to make sure that I made any little dream of his a priority.

I posted the video and hundreds of our friends and followers shared it, tagging Ellen DeGeneres, Lady Gaga, and Bradley Cooper in the hopes that somehow they would see it. The video didn't go viral, but it did reach a really nice guy from a local exclusive golf course. He was in charge of tending the grounds for many politicians and celebrities. He made it his mission to find a way for that video to reach Bradley Cooper. A couple days later, I was driving to the hospital when I received a text message from this very kid: *I did it!* It was immediately followed with an emailed video of Bradley Cooper recording a message to Dylan, encouraging him to continue to fight, to continue to try to work through the injuries that he had.

I was stunned. I couldn't wait to get to the hospital and see Dylan during one of his wakeful moments and share the video with him. He was awakened intermittently from the medically induced coma so his brain had time to adjust before being put under again. I was giddy with the excitement of a little girl at the idea that we had somehow made this happen for Dylan and maybe this would give him the motivation to keep on fighting for his life. That day, when I went into his room, he was sitting upright looking at me. "Dylan, you're never going to believe what I have to show you." I opened up my computer and started to play the video for him. Because his times of being wakeful were inconsistent, he was confused the first time he watched it. And so, I played it again. And he mouthed the words, "How the hell did you do this, Mom?"

His nurses gathered around, enamored with the sight of Bradley Cooper. And in that moment, it felt like we were local celebrities of a really good kind because we had accomplished a dream for our child and he had witnessed a message from a celebrity.

I've told you about all the practical things that our friends and community did for us, but there was something else beautiful and sacred about the community that we had around us. And that was a lot of believers in God. One of my friends spearheaded some prayer time where we would invite the community to come over and join in a group prayer, praying as a community for Dylan. This was something that happened several times over the course of his hospital stay and recovery.

I looked forward to the idea of a group of people gathering together to pray for our son and over our family. I don't remember many of the words that were said during those prayers, but there was one phrase that was used several times. It sits with me to this day. The prayer was repeated, that "God would show up and show off for our family," such unique and powerful words. These were the words that allowed me to continue to have faith that God was going to use our story to help other people, and that He was going to bless us in ways that I couldn't even fathom. There's not a day that goes by now where I don't ask God to continue to show up and show off for us.

Life Lesson: When we are going through difficult times, it can be challenging to see how we are still being supported (for example, how the community showed up for my family). Support may not come in the way we expect, but our needs can always be met.

Question: When was a time you and/or your family were struggling through difficult circumstances? Were your needs met? What was the outcome?

.

16

TRIGGERS AND CHILDHOOD

I had no idea that trauma I was facing as an adult would retrigger demons and trauma from the past. When I got the news that Dylan had crashed his car, I was scrambling for people to help me. My dad had always been the person to solve things. And so I reached out and alerted him to the crisis. Without hesitation, he jumped on a plane to be by my side. As a grown woman, I was still looking for someone to rescue me and to fix the situation.

There were two versions of my dad that I grew up knowing. One was loving and driven and problem-solving, and the other one was darkness. My father swooped in and began talking to doctors and nurses, trying to facilitate in Dylan's care. In the moments that we were at the hospital, I felt like I had another strong pillar to lean on, but at the same time, struggles from the past continued to be displayed. My father, having plenty of money to be able to afford a hotel right in Baltimore near the hospital, had made the decision to stay with a friend in the city instead.

He made sure to let us know that the accommodations were less than stellar as he struggled without air conditioning. He made a point of making sure that I knew this. It was like he needed me to know that this was hard on him, too.

I remember him once texting and calling me repeatedly while I was sitting bedside with Dylan. I couldn't answer my phone. So he proceeded to go through the list of people that he had met in those days, leading up to being with us, our friends and the community, calling them repeatedly. And then finally, when he couldn't reach anyone, calling the nurses' station, the very nurses who were helping to keep Dylan alive . . . for the petty question of where had he left his phone charger. It was a reminder, again, of my father being those two people. One was the guy who would sacrifice the shirt off his back for a stranger. The other, the sense of entitlement that his needs come before anyone else's. It stirred in me a struggle that made me feel sick, that he was in the space where my son was fighting for his life. I started to pull away and guard myself in an effort to be protected from his energy.

Around the same time that I made the phone call to my father, I made a similar call to my mother, who had spent decades in the background being married to my father. The quiet woman who was still processing the pain of losing her mother the year before.

I made the call and let her know what was happening to Dylan. I could feel her retreating to that quiet space she goes when life becomes too overwhelming. She wanted to make her support and presence known, but the level of what we were facing was something she couldn't bear. So she did little things to show her support that would keep her as far away from being bedside at the hospital as possible.

Late one afternoon, I returned from the hospital to find her in my kitchen with dinner. I looked at her from across the room and saw that she had on a necklace that I had never seen before.

Many years prior, my mother and I had a conversation about the things that I would want from my grandparents' home when they passed. I had one request. My grandparents had the longest lasting marriage of anyone I had known and somehow had overcome so many struggles, to love one another until death did them part. My grandmother's rings, her wedding set, were a powerful reminder of the bond that my grandparents had shared. A symbol to me of undying love.

"Mom, there's one thing that I want. Nana's rings."

And as I stood in the kitchen that day, looking at this curious necklace that wasn't very attractive, my mother saw my eyes catch on the attention of this new piece of jewelry. She put her arm around me and said, "Nana's wedding set couldn't be saved. So I had it made into this necklace. And one day it'll be yours."

We were standing right in front of the cutlery drawer. In that moment, I imagined if she had pulled a knife out from the drawer and stabbed me in the heart, it would've hurt less. You see, I didn't care about wearing the rings; I didn't care about the condition that they were in. It was the symbol of the love my grandparents shared that I wanted to cherish. I was willing to treasure those rings just in the palm of my hand occasionally to remind me that someone out there had accomplished something I had failed at repeatedly. They were a sign of hope, of everlasting love. And my mother had made a decision that those rings wouldn't be mine.

Both of my parents were bringing up pain within me

that was unbearable. I was already facing so much with my own child, with my own family, a situation between life and death. And here I was being faced with some of the demons from my past that I thought I had long since put to rest. I thought I had created boundaries to protect me from these toxic interactions with my parents. And yet reaching out to them during this time brought about the reminder of how far I still had to go.

I'm the oldest of three girls. And as sisters, as I've told you before, we weren't very close. Both of my sisters and I had a falling out several years earlier, and we had worked hard for forgiveness. We had worked hard to forage a new relationship of being friends, of moving past the toxic upbringing that we shared and redefining who we were. I formed an especially close bond with my sister Stephanie, who had spent years struggling with infertility. And when she finally found out that she was pregnant, she told me before she even told her husband.

We spent countless hours on the phone laughing with one another and talking about our futures and our healing journey. I was blessed enough to fly out to Arizona soon after her baby was born and spend a week loving on her as a new mom with a beautiful new gift in her life.

When Dylan crashed his car, my world stopped. And the relationships that I had worked so hard to cultivate took a back seat to anything else that was going on with Dylan. For Stephanie, I believe that she felt like I had abandoned her. Living across the country from each other, not being able to connect during that time caused our relationships to revert back to the same toxic style that we had growing up. I was failing my sister. I was in a crisis. And she had a new baby and needed my support.

The distance that we had worked so hard to overcome in order to cultivate closeness now became a crater with no other way to process it than to pull away. I realized I was still longing for the family upbringing to be different. I was still longing for a father who would be there and present, serving and not making it about himself. I was still longing for a mother to put her arms around me in support and not leave my side. And I was desperate for sisters who could forge a bond that would surpass our circumstances.

I don't remember sleeping much at all in those early weeks of Dylan's uncertain future. We tried staying in the Ronald McDonald House in the city, a space that was provided for by an organization all about connecting children with their parents who were in long-term hospital care, but both Mark and I were desperate for our own bed. So every morning, we would wake up really early and I would go and spend the entire day at the hospital, and then drive home and collapse in my bed where my mind would then try to solve all the world's problems as I stared at the ceiling. I was desperate for rest, for relief from the chaos, the trauma, and the pain. And yet each day I woke up, it felt like I was going deeper into the abyss of trauma, both from childhood and from my current circumstances.

Life Lesson: There are layers to healing. We may believe we have processed the life lessons from our past but as we face challenging circumstances, it can uncover programming and conditioning that pushes us to go deeper.

Question: Take a few moments to think about your current circumstances. Are there things happening that remind you of past events? Are you being impacted by the present or triggered by your past? What programming/conditioning that is no longer serving you do you need to surrender in order to heal?

17

I WAS UPSTAIRS

We don't think about the hospital being a spiritual place. We think of it as a place where people who are in pain go, but it *is* a very spiritual place. So many lives starting, souls entering the world, healing happening, and lives ending and leaving this earth. It became an environment of deep spiritual awakening for me. When you're at the hospital for an extended amount of time, you tend to see a lot of familiar faces in the space. There was a security guard who stood near the entrance of the hospital, a large, broad-shouldered African American man, who always had a smile on his face.

I remember passing by him frequently, but never making eye contact. In the early days of Dylan's injuries, everything was a blur, but this particular gentleman was a force that I felt every time I walked past him. One evening, we were descending in the elevator to leave the hospital, and that security guard was standing right at the doorway of the elevator when it opened. I made eye contact with him for the first time. There was an exchange that surpassed human words. I knew in that moment, as I looked into his eyes, that spiritually, we understood each other.

We had an entire conversation without speaking a word. I knew that he had similar intuitive abilities to mine. It was one of the first times where I remember knowing that someone understood me. I walked past him that day curious, but so absorbed in the pain of the experience I was going through that I didn't take much time to process it. A couple of days later, that same security guard was standing at the same spot outside the same elevator when we prepared to leave for the day.

And he stopped me.

"You are going to blow the doors off the church," he said.

I had no idea what he meant. And yet I wondered how he knew about the struggles I faced in my own journey, the battle between religion and spirituality, the desire to be true to who I felt I was called to be. I carried his words with me every day, wondering how exactly he saw me blowing the doors off the church. It was such a random thing to say and yet so pivotal, because I was at such a crossroads between being true to myself and following what I was taught. Dylan was in a medically induced coma. This meant that the doctors had control of how deep a sleep he was in. And they chose this approach because of the gravity of his injuries. Being in a medically induced coma allows the brain the ability to rest and to heal. When you get to a point where the healing has started to take place, the medical team will slowly wake you up from the coma intermittently.

Dylan would be awake for a few short moments before medical staff would readminister the medication that allowed him to be in the coma-like state and provide him space to heal. He was on a ventilator during this time and he had a trach. A tracheotomy keeps you from being able to speak words, but he was still able to mouth to us small little phrases letting us know that he was still there. During one of these short wakeful times, Dylan mouthed that he wanted to see our local pastor and his wife.

There was no request that Dylan could have made during this time that we wouldn't make every effort to see it happen. And so Mark and I reached out to Jim and Kristen and explained Dylan's request. They agreed to meet us at the hospital the next day. When we went home that night we collapsed in bed, as we did every night, after a long day at the hospital. And I remember lying in bed staring at the ceiling while listening to Mark gently snore next to me. I don't remember falling asleep. It felt like I was completely awake and alert.

The vision that I was about to have was life-changing. As I lay in bed listening to Mark's breathing, Dylan came walking into our room. He had on his white baseball cap, his gray hoodie, and his favorite pair of skinny jeans. He sat on the edge of the bed between Mark and me and flipped his hat around backward. "Mom, I don't know what to do because I've seen this." He pointed over toward the corner of my room and showed me this white light, so bright I couldn't even look directly at it.

I believe that light was God. And on one side of him was my grandfather; the other side was Mark's grandfather.

And then Dylan said, "But if I stay, I have a huge mess to clean up." He looked at me as if asking me what he should do. I don't know how I stayed so calm, but my breathing was peaceful.

"It's not up to me," I said. And then he was gone.

I don't remember falling asleep that night, but I know that I slept well. And when I woke up the next morning, I held a peace that far surpassed any understanding. As Mark got out of bed I started to recount to him the vision I had the night before. And before I could get out the entire story, he collapsed to his knees and started weeping. "Oh my God, Stacey, our son is going to die," he said. "He asked to see the pastor and his wife because he's going to die."

What I had found to be such a powerful experience that brought me so much peace led Mark to his knees in fear. We frantically got ready to go to the hospital, barely speaking the whole way there. As we made our way out of the parking garage onto the busy city, I heard Dylan's "voice" say to me, *Send Dad into the room, Mom. I'll confirm that I was there.*

Oh my God, I thought, *I have lost my mind. I must be so heavily medicated that I am talking to my son.* I heard him laugh. *"Mom, it's your time. I need you to send Dad in by himself. I'll prove that I was in your room."* Before I could think how crazy it sounded, I blurted out, "Mark, you have to go in when they wake Dylan up. He's going to confirm that he was in our room." Mark did look at me like I was crazy. And I felt like I *was* crazy, but we made our way through the hospital doors and up to the floor of Dylan's room.

As we entered the waiting room, there was the pastor, Jim, and his wife, Kristen, waiting for us. Here I was in a space with people who believed things were supposed to be done a certain way because of their religious indoctrination. And I had just had one of the most powerful experiences of my life. How was I going to explain to them the power of what had happened to me? Mark went back to Dylan's room and waited for the nurses to ease the IV medication that allowed his body to rest.

Fifteen minutes later, he came back out to the waiting room, tears streaming down his face. He nodded his head. "He confirmed it, Stacey. In two different ways he told me he was in our room last night."

"I told you," I said. "I told you he was in our room." There I was before Kristen and Jim explaining the power of the spiritual experience I had and knowing that no one could understand its gravity.

We made our way home from the hospital late like we did every day. And as we were climbing into bed and getting under the covers, the phone rang with the familiar number of the hospital. It was Dylan's nurse. "Everything is okay, please don't worry," she said. "But I needed to call you because we woke Dylan up tonight and he told us we needed to call you. He just keeps saying one thing over and over again. Maybe it'll make sense to you. He keeps saying 'I was upstairs. I was upstairs. I was upstairs.'"

When I got off that call, the peace that I had was something I hold even to this day. It wasn't about believing in a certain way, the things that I had been taught, the religious regimen of the way things should work. It was about trusting the vision that I had and honoring that vision for what it was, which was a gift from God. I received validation that I had a divine interaction that far surpassed this life and was one of the most profound spiritual experiences that I will probably ever have.

I was given the gift from Dylan of the validation that he had been in our room in that vision. And I knew that even if his life was shorter than what I had anticipated, that we'd had a divine experience that allowed us to know that if he crossed from this life to the next, there were divine beings waiting to welcome him into heaven.

· · ·

LIFE LESSON: Speaking our truth is important. Trusting our vision and believing it is from a higher place, regardless of others' judgments or opinions, is crucial.

QUESTION: Do you know what your gifts are? Are you using them or hiding them?

18

THE INFECTION

I don't know if there are words to describe a mother's love for her child, but I became profoundly aware that my connection with my son was so much deeper than I ever could have fathomed. When Dylan was a baby, he was the biggest and sickest baby in the NICU. His labor and delivery was a beautiful experience, but the moment he came out he struggled to breathe. I remember watching his little body fighting for life as an infant. You would think that experience would've prepared me for what was to come, watching him at seventeen as a much bigger kid fighting for his life.

There are so many things that the body experiences when it goes through a trauma. Dylan began to spike a fever between 106 and 107 degrees. Doctors reassured us that this was "normal for someone who had a traumatic brain injury." We watched his body fight for days. One morning, I entered Dylan's room, and it was one of the few times that no one other than my son and I were present. Usually there was a steady stream of nurses and doctors making rounds. I stood at the entrance of his dimly lit hospital room and watched his body wrapped in warming blankets, machines doing the breathing for him.

As I stood there watching him, I heard the words, *"Get the oil."* I remembered that amongst the many cards and well-wishes we had received, there was one card in particular that stood out. A neighbor of a client of mine had given her a small gauze of consecrated oil from the Saint Charbel. He was a healer in Lebanon in the 1800s. I placed my backpack on the chair next to Dylan's bed and rummaged through it to find *that* one card was the only card I had with me at the time. Inside it was the little plastic packet with the gauze soaked in oil.

I reached into the packet and pulled the gauze out. Dylan's body was breathing rhythmically by a machine. His eyes were closed and peaceful. My heart pounding, I placed the sanctified gauze across Dylan's temples, his forehead. I dabbed some oil next to the wound where the trach was inserted into his throat. And as I reached his chest, I began the powerful prayer of Reiki healing. I placed my hands over his chest and electricity coursed through my veins.

Before I could think about the words that I had just felt, I found myself running into the hallway. Dylan's nurse was standing right outside the room. "Nora," I said, "my son has a massive infection in his chest. He needs an IV antibiotic for three days and it starts with a C." She looked at me like I was insane. Maybe I was, but there was no time to think about putting the filter on and determining which things I was or wasn't supposed to say. All I could do was get the message out.

"Please call the doctors right now," I insisted before walking back into Dylan's room and collapsing in the chair next to his bed. What had I done? I had no medical training. I'm a hairdresser by trade. How was I going to speak this truth to the doctors? They were the experts; I was just his mom.

A few moments later, my cellphone rang and one of the doctors was on the other end. "I'll be honest with you," she said. "I've just completed a really long surgery and I'm exhausted. I hear you have some questions about your son."

"No," I said. "I don't have questions. I need you to come and look at my son right now. He has a massive infection in his chest."

"Okay," she said. "I'm on my way."

I hung up the phone and sat in silence, just me and Dylan's still body breathing with the rhythm of the machines, the beeping of the monitors playing in the background, as I waited for the experts to come and look at him. Within fifteen minutes, a team of doctors and nurses were surrounding Dylan's bed, realizing that they hadn't yet reviewed the scans taken a few hours before.

Dylan had a massive infection in his chest. One lung was completely filled with fluid and the other was nearly full. By the time we arrived at the hospital the next day, an IV bag was hanging next to his body with the antibiotic that started with a C. Later that day, we had a meeting around a large oval table in a conference room with the various teams of doctors who were in charge of saving the different parts of Dylan that were broken.

One doctor looked at me and said, "You know, you're weird, right?" And I chuckled. "But you also saved your son's life," he added. We sat around that oval table with all the specialists explaining to us the gravity of Dylan's various injuries, the plans for how they were going to take care of each part of his body from his head down to his toes. He had a specialist for his heart, for his lungs, for his liver, for his traumatic brain injury. And Mark and I sat quietly and listened to each doctor give a review of the treatment that would be needed to save him.

I remember a calm coming over me as they each explained the seriousness of what was happening with him and the possible options for treatment along with antici-pated complications. "I have something I need to say," I said. "I need you to promise me that if you can't save my son's life, that you'll save his organs, so that somehow his life will matter." The same doctor who came to look at Dylan, tired from a long surgery, looked me in the eyes with tears.

"In all the years that I've been caring for patients here, I've never heard these words come from a mother like they just came from you. I promise, no matter what, we'll make sure that your son's life matters."

There was a profound realization within all these expe-riences in the hospital. These moments of clarity and divine messages, intermixed with the most unbelievable pain, brought forth an understanding of who I was, who I am, and how I'm meant to show up in the world.

It took me back to that moment of standing in the base-ment salon sweeping hair with Mark when I had that nagging feeling that I was meant for more. I was reminded of the moments where I sat and listened to the podcast in the grocery store parking lot surrendering my idea of what I thought my life was going to look like for whatever God wanted it to look like. For the first time ever, I was trusting myself, trusting God, and listening to the divine messages that were being given to me.

In the darkest hours of my life, I was being given a clarity beyond my wildest dreams. I was finally showing up in the world exactly as I felt I was meant to. The bonus was that I was helping to save my son's life.

. . .

LIFE LESSON: There is a lot of noise around us but we are all receiving messages in some form. To embrace may require quieting our mind and connecting with our heart and soul. But when we take time to connect with our intuition, the messages can be life changing.

QUESTION: Do you take time to listen to your messages/intuition? When was the last time you listened to your intuition and how did it impact you?

19

SMACKED IN THE FACE BY REALITY

There were so many doctors involved in Dylan's care. He had a doctor for the broken bones, a team looking at his heart, his brain injury. Every aspect of his care had a team involved, giving a timeline for how long they thought it would be that he would need to recover. It was heartbreaking to watch my son go from a strong, capable football player, to losing thirty pounds in a matter of weeks, his body now frail and weak.

But the power of miracles was evident as the weeks passed and Dylan awakened more and began to heal. He blew all our minds with his progress. Within six weeks, he was standing upright in his room with two nurses helping him throw a ball back and forth to increase his mobility. Plans were made for Dylan to enter a local physical rehabilitation facility that would give him the structure that he needed to get his body moving again. His left knee was really injured. He shattered it and it had to be rebuilt. Learning to walk and move that knee again was imperative to his care.

We worked on making the arrangements for transport to the new facility, excited that soon he would be home. Something we anticipated taking months was happening much faster than any of us could have anticipated. He was taken by ambulance transport to the physical rehabilitation facility, where he entered into a room walking. He had a new set of caregivers at the facility, physical therapists who were supposed to help him regain his mobility. I have to believe now that there must have been some confusion in the treatment notes that went from the hospital to the rehab facility, because there's no other way I can come to terms with the next setback we faced.

Within three days of entering the rehab facility, Dylan's knee had been bent far beyond its capabilities, and he developed a large hematoma on his knee. I got up one morning preparing to go to the facility when Dylan phoned me. "Mom, I'm in so much pain," he cried. "I could walk just a couple of days before and no one is listening to me. I can't move my knee." I knew as his mom that part of my role was to advocate for him, but it never got easier to use my voice. Every time we were faced with a situation where I had to speak up, I would internally struggle, not knowing if the experts would even listen to me.

I walked into Dylan's room at the rehab facility to find his knee swollen and warm to the touch. I did the only thing that I knew to do; I walked in the hallway and called the top doctor at Shock Trauma who had been in charge of his care. "Doctor, you have to help my son. You saved his life and now he is in a bed again, unable to move." He brushed aside my concerns saying that it couldn't be that bad. And I continued to push for help.

Later that day, Dylan was transported by ambulance

back to Shock Trauma to receive another surgery to relieve his knee of that large hematoma. And we were back in the same routine that we had been so desperate to get out of: more surgery, more recovery, and Dylan crushed at the idea that he had taken a large step back. During this time, Dylan was on so many medications to control the pain that riddled his body. Our son, who had battled addiction for countless months prior, was now physically addicted to narcotics. The doctors knew that his body was physically addicted, and they also knew that he had an addiction history. The magnitude of his physical injuries left the doctors with no other choice but to medicate him. We had repeated meetings before leaving the hospital with his team and medical staff about how to properly medicate him as we brought him home. Though his mobility had increased, the bodily pain was still high. And the only way to manage it was to use some of the very same drugs that Dylan had been addicted to.

Once the knee surgery was complete, his recovery was rapid. I believe that the teenage boy who had spent the last several months in a hospital bed had the motivation to get back home. And that motivation allowed his body to heal so much faster than what any of us could have expected.

Finally, Dylan's release day arrived and he was headed home. This brought an all-new challenge. We had downsized from the typical large family minivan to smaller vehicles as our children had gotten older and started driving. There was no way for us to comfortably and safely transport Dylan home in one of these smaller vehicles. Thankfully, we were blessed with yet another angel, a close friend of Mark's, who effortlessly took in the smaller vehicle that we had. And without even seeing it, we purchased a brand new minivan. We were able to bring our son home and begin the next phase of his healing journey.

I HAD BEEN SO focused on Dylan's recovery in the hospital that I didn't fully absorb the adjustments and implications of bringing him home. The meetings that we had with medical staff before leaving the hospital covered all areas that we might anticipate when we got home. "It's imperative that you know that if your son uses after these injuries his body has been through, it will likely kill him," they pointed out. Even recounting this now makes my blood run cold. I felt like my son was a ticking time bomb, and bringing him home was a huge responsibility and somewhat terrifying. We converted our living room, the space where we had spent so many family gatherings, into a makeshift bedroom for Dylan. For long distances, he still required a wheelchair. But for shorter distances, like getting around our home, he used crutches. Having him on the main floor of the house was the only way we were going to be able to navigate this successfully.

I had no idea what it would look like to become a full-time caregiver, but I actively started creating a schedule and a routine. Everything from distributing medications to arranging home healthcare nurses and physical therapy was my responsibility.

When you bring home an addict from the hospital whose body is physically addicted to the narcotics that he's been on for months, the only way to be safe is to have those medications in a lockbox, with a key. I felt like a prison warden, monitoring everything about my son. His body would start to show symptoms of withdrawal if I was even minutes delayed in distributing those meds from the lock-box. Every day, every hour was governed by the strict schedule we followed for distributing his medications. Between administering, life became about changing dressings, breathing exercises, and everything that we could possibly do to cultivate a stronger version of Dylan.

Dylan's friends were ecstatic at the idea of him being home. They pleaded with us for opportunities to see him. I hoped his friends coming around and spending time with him would trigger memories of better days and motivate him to keep on going. So, I readily agreed to visits from the football team and friends from school. Soon, a stream of visitors showed up at our door and I would welcome them in. But first I would pull them aside for an intimate conversation. "I need you to know that if Dylan uses again, he could die," I'd warn. I wanted them to feel the gravity of what his body had been through as a warning. I wanted them to know that if they engaged in any of those activities with Dylan again, that he might not survive it.

Typical of teenagers, they think they're indispensable, that nothing can stop them. And on one occasion, a couple of Dylan's friends from the football team came over to hang out and spend the night. We found out later that they brought alcohol with them and proceeded to drink with our son still recovering. I can't make sense of how that decision played out, why they thought that was an acceptable thing to do. I'm grateful that Dylan made it through that time, but I often wonder how much further it could have gone.

While so much of this story has been about Dylan, I must think about the impact it had on our other kids. Even in the telling of the story, they've been put on the back burner.

Katelynn was finally establishing her independence as a

woman, a girlfriend, and a flourishing business owner. But any time that her siblings needed her, she was there, even putting most of her life on hold during this difficult time for Dylan and our family. She showed up in a way that even now blows my mind. At the tender age of twenty-one, she was a second mom to all her siblings, loving on them and doing all she could to keep our family together.

Aydan, just two years younger than Dylan, was in the middle of his high school career. After Dylan's crash, everyone at school wanted to know what happened with his brother. The stress of it all impacted Aydan greatly. He wanted desperately for things to return to normal, yet the community wouldn't allow him the experience of going to school without sensitive questions about his big brother, the varsity football player.

When it became too much, we were blessed to have another angel come into our life who homeschooled her own children. She was a client of mine and a friend. She asked if I would consider homeschooling Aydan, then quickly agreed to facilitate in leading him on the best journey possible for his education. She brought him into her family home and gave him a space that was safe and loving during a time that felt so uncertain. The idea of homeschooling Aydan, such a social and happy child, felt like maybe I was depriving him of the experience of high school in our local school. And yet a calmness overtook him when he left school and didn't have to be in that environment anymore.

Eastyn was still so young, only in kindergarten at the time. How do you explain the seriousness of a situation like ours to a five-year-old? Each day that Eastyn went to school, both the teachers and the school nurse would rally around her offering hugs and support and encouragement.

There were so many milestone events that I missed during this time because I was at the hospital so much with Dylan. And yet these women made sure that Eastyn never felt deprived of having a loving person there supporting her.

We continued to feel the blessings of our community rallying around us in ways that we didn't even know we would need support.

I tried hard to include my parents and my siblings in the updates of what was happening in our life, but I was in survival mode. All my energy was going into being a caregiver and a nurse. Every day, when I woke up, my focus was: what time did I have to distribute medications? What time are the home healthcare nurses coming? Who will be dropping off a meal today? Has Dylan done his breathing exercises? I felt like I didn't even have time to parent my other children. Issues with my parents and my siblings became an added stress that I no longer had space for. Ultimately, I made the decision to send them an email, stating: "I can't do this anymore. The challenges that I'm facing within my own family are overtaking me and I need space."

I've continued to keep that space for the last three years. It was the only thing I knew to do to emotionally fortify myself. I had to do everything I could to help my son, and then I needed to start helping myself.

LIFE LESSON: When life throws us a curveball like a crisis, we can go into survival mode. But when we neglect ourselves, it has a ripple effect on all areas of our life. Even during difficult times, taking a little bit of time for self-care can have a massive impact on ourselves and those around us.

. . .

QUESTION: How are you making yourself a priority? What can you do today for you?

20

MY HEALTH MATTERS

A t the start of the issues with Dylan, I was more aligned than I had ever been in mind, body, and spirit. I had established so many good habits that created a lifestyle for me of optimal health. But after Dylan's crash, all those healthy habits stopped. The meal planning that I would do to make sure my body had the nutrients it needed was replaced with long days at the hospital, sustaining on snacks, convenient fast food, and junk from the vending machines. I'd return home every night to a bag of Mega Stuf Oreos that I would eat until I felt nauseous.

There was little time for sleep. During the day, I was a caregiver, and as soon as my head hit the pillow at night I would replay and evaluate every single scenario, leading up to where we were. Three weeks after Dylan's crash, I was exhausted, lost, and knew that I needed to reach out for help. I scheduled an appointment with my doctor. She was already aware of the situation happening within our home because of the small community we live in. I told her about my sleep deprivation and wept in the office while I told her about the schedule that I had been trying to keep up with caring for Dylan.

She recommended I go on some medication that would help me with the anxiety and sleep. It was a medication I was familiar with when facing postpartum depression after Dylan was born. At that time, a psychiatrist promised that the medications they were putting me on would help, but they rendered me a zombie unable to function. I had flashes of going through that same zombie-like demeanor again through this challenge with Dylan. For me, it didn't feel like the right decision, but how was I going to continue in survival mode? What support was I going to give my body to be able to function through this time, to be the caregiver I needed to be, that I was required to be?

There are so many conversations that happen when you're a hairdresser working with clients behind the chair. I had several clients who, in confidence, talked about their use of medical marijuana. One client in particular struggled with my same issues with anxiety. She said her life was much better because of medical marijuana. Now I know what you're all thinking. How could a mother whose child was battling addiction even contemplate the idea of using medical marijuana? My friends, it was definitely a conflicting decision. I had lost my health physically, mentally, and emotionally. I had lost my business and I had nearly lost my child. I was on the brink of losing myself. I knew that I needed to find a way to function.

Shortly after the doctor's visit, I made the decision to try medical marijuana for the first time. I can remember the day very clearly. It was the first time that I slept more than a couple of hours. I woke up the next day feeling the most rested I had been since learning of Dylan's crash. I was able to show up for Dylan's various appointments. I was able to be a little bit more present for my kids. It went against everything I had believed in for so long. Drugs had riddled several of my relationships. My husband had struggled with his own addictions and now my son was struggling with his. The decision to pursue something that was so controversial felt like something I had to hide.

I was secretive with my family, mainly my kids, out of fear of judgment and being unsure of how *I* even felt about the decision. I would retreat to the bathroom and smoke privately before returning to my daily tasks. I needed to show up; I needed to be a caregiver. Somehow I had to find the way to navigate through the most traumatic experience of my life. I began the journey of regularly using medical marijuana edibles along with occasional smoking. Honestly, I don't know how I would've gotten through that time without this tool. It was used like a medicine, never abused. With it, I was able to continue going to the hospital every day, talking to doctors, helping to make decisions for Dylan's care. Going forward, I was able to bring him home and be his caregiver because I was finally getting a little bit of sleep and eating properly.

I never imagined facing such a personal decision. Raised in a home that was drug- and alcohol-free, I had navigated through relationships with multiple addicts. And here I was, a mother, fighting for her child and making a decision that felt so deeply conflicting to my foundational beliefs. Despite initial reservations, it calmed my racing thoughts, allowing me to be the mother and the caregiver that I needed to be for my son.

· · ·

LIFE LESSON: One's journey is deeply personal. We need to make decisions that are in our highest good, regardless of what others think.

QUESTION: How do the opinions of others impact you? How has that impacted you in your day-to-day life?

21

LETTING GO

Well before everything started with Dylan, I had met with my gynecologist and was aware that I would need a surgery to fix problems I had been struggling with since the birth of my fourth child. I opted to have a voluntary hysterectomy in September of 2019, only five months after Dylan's crash. I knew that I could no longer ignore the impact of my physical ailments.

As I was trying to recover from this surgery, Dylan made it clear that he wanted life to resume as normal as possible. He was struggling with the restrictions of his physical health compounded with the restrictions of living back at home. In October, he came to me and expressed his desire to go to a party with all his friends. Internally, I wondered how he thought he could go to a party where there would absolutely be substances he would be tempted to use.

"Dylan, how are you going to go to a party and stay sober?" I asked.

"I can do it, Mom," he said. "I just want to be with my friends."

There are times as a parent when you want to hold on as tightly as possible. This was one of those times. And yet I knew now, at the age of eighteen, he had the right to make whatever decisions he wanted, whether I agreed with them or not. He went to that party and came home the next day. I was lying in bed resting, still in so much physical pain. I asked if he had used and he admitted that he had. "Dylan, there is no way that we can continue to care for you if you're not willing to care for yourself," I said. He abruptly packed a few belongings in his car and drove away from the house.

My heart dropped into my stomach. Now my son was not only a young adult who was battling mental health and substance abuse issues, but he was a child with major medical concerns. Mark and I waited throughout the day, wondering if Dylan was going to return. We happened to have a locator on our phone where we could track the location of our children, and on this day it was a huge blessing. When we tracked Dylan's location, he was at a seedy motel in a town nearby, a place known to house prostitutes and addicts.

We drove quietly to the motel's location, hoping we would be able to find our son before any detrimental decisions were made on his part. We circled the perimeter of the motel searching for his car to no avail. We asked the front desk manager if he could tell us what room our son was in. He looked at us like we didn't belong there and said that was information he wasn't allowed to give. But we pleaded with him about the gravity of our son's medical condition and he reluctantly told us which room he was staying in.

We drove around the back of the motel, spotted his car and pulled into the space next to it. "What do we do?" I asked Mark. We waited and waited and waited.

While we sat in the car, we contacted local authorities to see if they would come and assist us in the process of once again attempting to save our son. Several police cars and a crisis counselor came within minutes, banging on the door of Dylan's motel room. It felt like forever as we waited for him to answer. The crisis counselor strongly encouraged that we wait in a spot where Dylan would not be able to see his anxious parents. Police banged on the door for several minutes, and finally it opened. There was Dylan, impacted by whatever substance he had chosen that day, insistent that he was okay and he had no desire to get any help. His eyes were glazed over and distant. He was void of any emotion.

I became profoundly aware that I was not in control. I recognized very deeply that I wanted my son to live more than he did. We drove away from the motel that day leaving our son behind, tears streaming down both of our faces. In the weeks that followed, the manipulation of our son's addiction and his addictive behavior became apparent. He began couch surfing from one place to another, playing off people's desire to help him convincing others that his parents had left him no other options.

The kindness of so many strangers who were now engrossed in our story became the way Dylan survived the next several months. The manipulative tactics of his addictive behavior became an avenue for Dylan to find places to stay and continue using, lying, and plummeting into further addiction. Many people in the community questioned our parenting, some of them even our own family members. The perception was that we had abandoned our son, thrown him out on the street and left him to navigate this journey on his own.

During this already emotional and painful time, my health continued to suffer. The relief that I thought I would experience from the surgery in September didn't arrive. I spent the better part of three months suffering with pain that felt like razor blades in my pelvis. I repeatedly returned to the doctor's office expressing the level of the pain I was in and was handed prescriptions for narcotics. My doctor and other close friends gently nudged me to believe that the physical pain I was in was a manifestation of the pain I was experiencing with my son. Internally, I knew something was very wrong but I had to question my judgment because of everything already happening in my life. *Was I crazy?* Was Dylan's pain impacting me so much that it was causing my own physical pain?

I was blessed yet again with other angels in my life, people who had medical knowledge. When I explained to them the seriousness of my pain, they gave me the name of another surgeon to go and have a consult with. After spending three months in bed barely functioning while Dylan left for another rehab stint, I went in to see this new doctor. She looked at the scans of what I had done and the tools that were used to perform the surgery and immediately she had a solution. Part of my uterus had been left in my body. Another surgery was the only option to relieve me of the pain that had nearly crippled me. In December of 2019, three months after the original surgery, I went back into the hospital and received a surgery that relieved me of my pain and allowed me to move forward.

During the time of waiting for this surgery to happen, I became physically addicted to pain killers. The surgeon who performed my original surgery had me convinced that the pain I was in could only be managed with narcotics. I never imagined my body physically addicted to a medication . . . and yet here I was, battling my own demons and facing the symptoms of withdrawal as I moved away from the painkiller and into healing. People assumed I was still mourning, that during those three months, the pain that my son was experiencing and the gravity of the shift in our family was the reason that I was laid up in bed. Advocating for my own health, after recognizing that my body was speaking to me and I needed to listen, was crucial yet again. It was time for me to speak my truth, but this time I was an advocate for myself, not my son.

My entire focus began to be a realization that I could not help Dylan. I had to save myself. In the time that he needed me so desperately, I put every ounce of my being into his care and into helping him survive. Inadvertently I had lost myself. My poor physical health was the final blow to recognize that I had to save myself.

LIFE LESSON: We are not here to fix people, not even our own children. Ultimately it is up to us to save ourselves. When you get on an airplane to take a flight, the flight attendants always encourage you in the event of an accident to place your own oxygen mask on first, before your child's. It's our responsibility to save ourselves.

QUESTION: Have you ever lost yourself in another's person pain? Do you try to fix people or guide them?

22

RECONNECTING WITH ME

Once I'd recovered from the second surgery, I felt more energized, motivated to return to work. My responsibilities as a hairdresser had been on the back burner for too long. It was time to return to life as "normal," and yet nothing felt the same. Months of being away from the chair, not exercising, and focusing on Dylan, had left me heavier than I had been in years. The busy schedule of clients I once had was gone. People I had spent decades loving on and caring for behind the chair had moved their needs elsewhere. Could I truly blame them for *my* absence?

But to be honest, I felt hungry for something else, some sort of fulfillment, maybe even a distraction. Three months into returning to work, our world was hit by a major pandemic: COVID-19. Life as I knew it, again, came to a screeching halt. Days passed by with no real structure, no consistency, no schedule. During this time, while exploring on social media, I stumbled upon a woman who was doing a makeup tutorial. I've always loved makeup. Taking the time every morning to put myself together, looking in the mirror and applying different colors and shades, was very therapeutic from the time I was a young teenager. It was a way to show up for myself every day, a meditative process that always brought me so much peace.

The woman I stumbled upon, on social media, was with a network marketing company, and though I wasn't thrilled about the idea of network marketing, I loved the idea of using quality products and enjoyed the art of creating. The price to start was very reasonable, so I decided to jump in and become a part of the Farmasi family. Their beauty products were inexpensive and made with quality ingredients. And as soon as my promotional kit arrived, I decided to pass the time during COVID by doing my own makeup tutorials using Farmasi's products on Facebook Live. I became a brand ambassador for the company, making money off the sales I received from the women who watched the live presentations and purchased products from me. I was creating a business simply by sharing my love for makeup and beauty.

When I first got on camera, I was awkward and nervous, but also excited to have a distraction, something to do to pass the time. Waking up every morning without a schedule was challenging, but when it came to showing up for my makeup tutorial videos, it gave me something to look forward to every single day, a sense of purpose. During a time when people were feeling so isolated, I began to connect with a community of women who were excited about my on-camera conversations about self-love and self-care. I even decided to pull out some oracle cards during one of my videos. I got brave in sharing my abilities, not only to learn to love myself and care for myself, but to add in some of the intuitive gifts that I had been given.

It was one of the first times that I was publicly confirming my abilities and people were responding. From the month I started promoting Farmasi's products, I began to earn a solid paycheck. Money missed from not seeing salon clients became a distant memory because it was replaced by my ability to show up every day doing something I loved. The response from women on Facebook Live was an outpouring of support and a desire to join me on the journey. It sparked a following I didn't know I needed at a time when my healing was so crucial. By showing up every day on camera, encouraging women to love on themselves, and to care for themselves, I was reminding *myself*, too, of the importance of self-love and self-care.

By sharing parts of what was happening in my personal life and allowing people to see my soul, I was on my own journey to healing. And I wasn't waiting until I was healed. I put myself out there—broken, overweight, and recovering —to create space for other women to show up just as they were. I created a platform based off my journey and allowed myself the freedom to creatively express exactly who I was. I was beginning to be seen. I was sharing my story and using my abilities to not only love others, but to finally love myself.

LIFE LESSON: Making self-care a priority not only has a massive impact on us, it creates a positive effect on those around us. When we make our own needs a priority, we are better equipped to face whatever circumstances come our way. And it ensures we are showing up as the best version of ourselves.

. . .

QUESTION: What is your self-care routine? What can you implement today to prioritize your needs?

23

NOT JUST A HAIRDRESSER

I continue to be amazed at the way God shows up and shows off. After months spent building my business with Farmasi, getting on camera every day to encourage women to love themselves, I got riddled with a nasty stomach bug. On day one of a three-day stint in bed, I was contacted by a friend who said, "Hey, Stacey, there's a new social media app called Clubhouse. I think it's perfect for you."

While confined to bed battling the stomach pains, I started exploring this audio app called Clubhouse where people from all around the world would talk on all different topics. The app allowed me to go into virtual "rooms" of people and take part in discussions. I found another way to use my voice. It lit a fire in me. The platform allows participants to either listen in to a discussion or participate by speaking. Soon I found myself going "on stage" and speaking my story, our family story, for the first time. During my hours on Clubhouse, I stumbled upon a community who was focused on using our voices to make an impact. A whole new world of people aligned with the vision of making the world a better place opened up to me.

Most notably, I met two beautiful women from the UK, Amanda and Rosie, who both were focused on their life coaching businesses for women. The three of us aligned together to create a self-love course called Know Your Worth, where we would help other women to take actionable steps to loving themselves. The very thing that I had struggled with for so many decades of my life was now something I helped other women cultivate within themselves. It inspired me to get my life purpose life coaching certification. I had no idea what was next but I was very aware that I had spent so many years behind the chair coaching people, loving on them, and advising them. Why couldn't I do that in a different way?

While on Clubhouse, I also met some amazing spiritual healers. It continued to feed the fire in me that I didn't know existed, sparking a level of healing I was so desperate for but had no idea how to navigate. As I got on the "stage," sharing the story of our family—the pain, the heartbreak, and the trauma—people started taking an interest and wanted to know more. I began getting offers to speak on a couple of different podcasts as a guest to share the story of moving from pain into purpose. (Looking back, I was still in the pain trying to *find* the purpose.)

But the more that I spoke and shared the journey of our healing, of our pain, I realized God was going to use our story in a much bigger way than I could ever have imagined. People were listening intently to hear the lessons I had learned through the process. "Stacey, you really need to write a book" became a common refrain. I have ADD (attention deficit disorder) and the idea of writing a book seemed very overwhelming. I couldn't wrap my head around the idea of organizing my thoughts and recounting the series of traumatizing, life-changing events. But I happened to connect with somebody on Clubhouse who was a writing coach. He offered to help me write my book. I set up regular sessions with him, paying him to attempt to help me organize my thoughts and share my story. I began actively pursuing the process of documenting the journey of our family, and turning it into purpose.

As I tried to write the book, I found it going in a direction that didn't feel aligned with the story unfolding. Now, with time and space, I can see that the story was still being written. But in the moment, I felt discouraged and frustrated. How was I going to take this story and help impact the lives of others?

I gave up on the book. I stopped trying because it felt like I was fighting up against another brick wall that I didn't have the energy to battle.

IN ALL THE years that I've spent working with people, both behind the chair and through my healing practice, I've become profoundly aware that there's only one thing that everyone has in common. Everyone has experienced pain.

Our pain may all look different, some of us going through life-altering, painful situations, while others might only experience the pain of a broken bone. But everyone has pain. It's a choice to heal it. I made a conscious decision to take my pain and turn it into purpose. I knew that everything I had gone through had some kind of deeper meaning to it. Actively pursuing the clarity of the deeper meaning was the only thing that relieved the pain of the experiences of the past several years. And the more I spoke about it, the more clarity I gained. As I navigated through the virtual hallways of Clubhouse, visiting all its "rooms" of different topics and diverse people, I still felt like there was something missing. There needed to be a club on Clubhouse where people could gather and have conscious conversation—soul-centered, heartfelt conversation.

And so, I decided to create my own club. Many, many years ago, I had a vision. I saw this hub, a center, where people would go and have various needs met (e.g., holistic practices, self-care, self-love, exercise), a place for people to authentically be themselves to heal.

Soul Center was born, my fifth baby. Soul Center was a virtual space focused on authenticity and vulnerability, a safe place for people to come and share their journey to healing and give insight that could inspire others to awaken on their own journey.

I fell in love with the idea of inspiring other people on their journey to a deeper meaning of life. Finally, I was using my voice in a way that impacted others. As I shared my story even more, it was preparing me for the process of finally writing this book. Yes, there were still steps—or chapters—ahead in my healing journey, more stumbling and lessons to learn along the way. In truth, it never really ends. But I continued every day to show up in Soul Center with a team of people who were working together to awaken others on their journey to healing and find the purpose in their pain.

The club attracted a lot of attention. People wanted to be a part of the team. I was excited about working with a group of people who were aligned, but I had little knowledge of being a leader. I had spent most of my career in the beauty industry navigating my business as a solo entrepreneur. The excitement of people wanting to follow and align with my vision was something new and exciting.

I allowed that excitement to be the driving force, allowing anyone who wanted to participate to be a part of things. I completely overlooked going deeper into evaluating where each one of these people was in their own healing journey. In hindsight, forming a team of people requires so much more than the desire to be a part of something bigger, especially when it comes to deep spiritual work and healing. And, though all these new friends were well-intentioned, it would soon become clear we were in disparate phases of our journeys. Though Soul Center was a space to include everyone, the team leading it needed to be aligned in the vision, and willing to work on their own personal goals to living a soul-centered existence. Between the rapid growth, and the unfamiliar new position of leadership, I was unaware that this newly forming team was missing some of the key components it would require to thrive.

LIFE LESSON: Everyone has a story to tell, a life lesson that others can learn from. When we share our experiences and how we grew/expanded from them, it helps others who may face something similar.

QUESTION: What life lessons have you experienced that helped you and could help others?

24

MANIFESTING MY DREAMS

S oul Center started to form quite a following. We had regular rooms, multiple days a week. We would host discussions on spiritual topics. One day, while I was leading a room, someone unknown to me entered the room and heard me speaking. He came up "on stage" to ask me a few questions about my story and offer encouragement. Nimesh and I developed a friendship quickly. He would come into the club and challenge me with thought-provoking, expansive questions. I look back now and realize he was challenging me to see the purpose in the pain I was sharing. And while on the stage, during one of our regular conversations that was publicly displayed in the Clubhouse room, he asked me what I wanted to manifest.

The idea of manifesting something was a thought that hadn't entered my mind in the last several years. In fact, the last time I was manifesting it was my basement salon space. My life had been all about survival. And here I was on a public platform being asked about my dreams. Before I could even think of it, I said to Nimesh, "I want to visit you in the UK. I want to manifest a trip to London."

I'm not a world traveler. I've spent so much time in relationships having children, and started so young. The idea of me taking a trip like this was completely foreign. And exhilarating. As soon as I said those words, I began the process of researching when I could come to the UK and how I would make it happen. I reached out to my friend, Diane. "Hey, you want to go on an adventure?" I asked. "Why don't we go to the UK?" As crazy as it was, we started looking at flights and dates. Diane would be able to join me for part of the trip, and then I would be flying solo. There were so many details to work out in the planning, including child care for Eastyn and making sure Mark could cover those responsibilities while I was gone.

It was an incredible experience. I spent eleven days exploring a part of the world I had never seen before and connecting with people I had only met through a social media app. I had spiritual experiences, like visiting my first Hindu temple. I'll never forget sitting on the temple floor which had a beautiful lotus flower in the center of it. I sat cross-legged, surrendering to the moment and allowing myself to feel what it's like to truly be living again. My entire focus on the trip was to connect with as many souls as I could that I had connected with on Clubhouse.

I spent days wandering London and seeing so many sites and tapping into a part of me that I felt I'd lost. Nimesh had an incredible mentor named Sidra Jafri. He spoke of her often on this trip, telling me about her life and the lessons that they had learned from her before she left this earth. I listened to those stories and the impact that this woman had, but it wasn't until the last day of my trip that I connected with her.

Nimesh and I sat on his sofa looking through Sidra's work. And as he placed a notebook on my lap of her notes, her hard work sitting before me, I felt a deep, energetic connection with her soul. While we sat there, Nimesh asked, "When are you coming back to the UK?"

I hadn't even thought about coming back to the UK. I let the question sit with me as I anxiously prepared for the first time to be flying internationally by myself. I've spent so much of my life leaning into another for support, whether it was my father or my husband, always feeling that there was someone there to carry me along when something felt too challenging. The idea of navigating an international flight in a big airport by myself felt so overwhelming, but the power in conquering my fear was empowering.

I landed at Dulles Airport hours later. And soon after the flight landed, I was picked up by my friend Diane. I loaded my suitcase into the trunk of her car. Before I even put on my seat belt, I blurted out, "I'm going back to the UK. I'm going back in January and I'm staying for a month."

"What?" Diane said, turning to face me with a bewildered look, ignoring the traffic behind us.

I started to laugh. And then, I immediately picked up the phone and called Nimesh. "I think I'm coming back to the UK," I told him. "I think I'm meant to be there for a month." Without hesitation, he welcomed the idea of me coming and staying with him.

I had no idea what was next. I was simply listening to my intuition and trusting that there was something more I was supposed to gain from my time in the UK. I recognize now that I was walking into my truth as a healer and saying goodbye to my life as a hairdresser. It felt like God was providing me with a way to move forward using my gifts and my story to impact others, to help them find a way through their pain and to cultivate healing. I was doing another trust fall.

LIFE LESSON: When we are manifesting, it's important to be clear on what we are trying to manifest and take actions toward it. When we want to experience miraculous things, it's important that we get out of our comfort zone and do things that expand us.

QUESTION: What do you dream of doing? What would you do if fear were not a factor? How are you holding yourself back from the life that you want?

25

THE MAGIC OF MERLIN

After the epiphany that I would be returning to the UK for a second time, I found myself faced with the task of talking to my family. How was I going to explain that I was leaving for a trip for the longest time I had ever been away from them, with no real vision of what I was going to create?

I knew I was working on building something, but I was unclear what it was, another trust fall. I had a deep connection with Sidra, Nimesh's mentor, and my feeling was that somehow what I was doing was connected with her. So, when I approached my family, I simply said, there's a healer who has passed from this realm who's left an impact. I think I'm meant to study her. After a few conversations and some planning, they reluctantly supported my decision with no real understanding of what it was I was going to create. My single-minded focus on finding myself outweighed any resistance I faced from family members. Though they did not understand what I was creating, they supported me in making my vision a reality.

Since the age of eighteen, I have never taken time to focus on my own dreams and goals without the responsibility of other people, whether it was a husband or children. My focus was always on my family. The idea of abandoning all these responsibilities for a month seemed crazy, and yet it seemed destined.

I began planning the trip, booking my plane ticket and making other arrangements, only to have chaos strike again.

Mark received a diagnosis of COVID, and here I was faced with yet another decision. The funny thing was Nimesh and I had only spoken the week before, expressing how excited we were that I would be making this trip.

"Maybe you'll come early," he said.

"Nimesh, the only way I'm coming early is if all my clients are canceled."

And as luck, or unluck, would have it, Mark got COVID and my clients were all canceled. My anxiety was through the roof. If he was sick, how was I going to make the trip? I hid isolated in my room, frantically making plans and packing as I went. I had a single-minded focus. This trip felt pivotal in my healing journey. Even seeing my partner struggling with illness would not stop me. I was on a mission to save myself.

Changing my flights was a nightmare. Travel during the COVID-19 pandemic is hassle enough, but figuring out last minute changes just added to my anxiety of this new season. For instance, who knew that you couldn't get an Uber from my house in rural Maryland? It was clear the universe was constantly expanding me. I was being pushed farther and farther out of my comfort zone. Thankfully, with Nimesh's support, I was able to figure out how to navigate the transportation.

I spent so much time wondering how this trip was going to play out, and yet with every step I took, there was an answer. I made it to the UK earlier than expected, my bags haphazardly packed in my rush to make it away from the house without getting COVID. But I knew that this was where I was meant to be.

Nimesh's home was given the name Merlin by his late mentor, Sidra. It's a healing space, a sacred place. On my first journey there, I knew it was a place where lots of healing had happened, not only for me, but for others. And so I had this nervous excitement about being in Merlin again and experiencing the healing powers of this safe space.

Merlin felt like Heaven, a place I could only imagine in my dreams that somehow God gave me the blessing of experiencing yet again. The gift of this beautiful space was quiet to focus further on my vision for myself and for Soul Center. Soul Center was no longer an idea that was birthed on Clubhouse, but something I wanted to expand into spreading light and helping others on their healing journey. It became very clear that I wanted to inspire people to align with their soul's purpose. Being there in Merlin, in that sacred space, allowed me the opportunity to cultivate that vision into something tangible, something I could bring and show to other people, allowing them the opportunity to be a part of the community and to carry the vision forward. Up until this point, Soul Center was a Clubhouse club with a vision and no structure. While at Merlin, Nimesh and I began to create a structure to this vision. He began to play a more active role in helping me take my ideas and form them into a tangible plan. We spent hours around the kitchen table, brainstorming and cultivating a concrete layout for the way we would run the club, and setting goals for how we were going to serve this growing community. We channeled a mentorship program to help people who are in the process of their awakening.

I began to see that Soul Center was a way of life. I became increasingly motivated to cultivate this way of life into a brand and a business that would allow me to do the deeper healing work with people who were ready to make the changes needed to live a life awakened. And, I began to wonder if some of the team I was working with were not willing or ready to do the work required to set an example for those who were coming into the space seeking answers.

It was also the deepest way of honoring Nimesh's late mentor. Her greatest desire was to carry forth the healing tools that she had learned through her own process. It was as if she had taken the baton in a relay race and passed it on to me. This was an opportunity for me to go through my next level of healing and bring that gift to other people. I finally found my voice.

My power came from speaking my truth, and I found it in a space far away from home, where I was able to be held and loved on and my cup was running over. I've worked as a business owner for so many decades, but I've always done it alone, finding that the best way for me to execute the vision of caring for my clients was to do it solo. Now I've been learning about becoming a leader, about providing a space where people can feel that there is someone who is leading them to a greater vision for themselves and for the world.

I was becoming a leader to Soul Center and to so many people who came into the space wanting to have more clarity on their own healing journey. Remember my closet and the power of that healing space? The space that once held so much pain became where I provided healing for others and, in turn, healing for myself. Many times when I would do my Clubhouse rooms, I would go into that now sacred space and allow those hearing my voice the opportunity to experience the blessing of its healing portal.

For so long, I believed that my closet was the only safe space for me to process pain and to help people heal. I was very nervous about leaving my closet and heading to the UK because that had been the space where I had provided so many people the clarity that they needed on their journey. What if I couldn't re-create that portal? But as I embarked on my journey to the UK, I found that I brought my closet's power with me, that the sacred portal I believed only existed in a dark cluttered corner of my house, was something inside me, something I carry wherever I go.

As I stepped away from my environment where so much pain had happened, it gave me the space to heal on another level. It prompted me to realize that the tugging of my heartstrings to write a book were still there. There was no way I could leave the UK without making this book happen. The desire to share the depths of the pain and turning it into purpose now felt like a mission.

I KNEW this trip to the UK was all about working, but while there in this beautiful space, I had the experience of magic in all different kinds of places. Each played a part in my healing.

One of the beautiful places that I experienced was Minack Theatre. Minack Theatre was initially a dream in one woman's eyes to create a beautiful space where people could come and experience the magic by the water in a man-made beautiful space. She was undeterred by the many obstacles that got in her way, knowing her vision had to be made a reality. It felt so similar to the feelings that I had of creating an international space for healing.

One night I got to enjoy the beauty of Cirque du Soleil. Thinking that I was just going to enjoy the beauty of a show and the fun of a night out on a town, I was delighted to receive divine messages. Every single one of the performers has to work in perfect sync to execute each one of the magical things that they did on that stage. At one point, three men took turns throwing a woman up into the air with the most incredible acrobatics. And every time they caught her, she did the trust fall.

The messages were clear. I was on the path and the signs were everywhere.

My focus was on creating a vision and a foundation for what was to come. The desire to write a book never left. But being away from home gave me a space to process the story, to revisit all the emotions, the pain, the heartache, the trauma. It also allowed me the opportunity to walk the journey, to tell the story, to feel it again, and process all the lessons that came along with this gut-wrenching part of my journey.

I spent a month away from home, completely focused on myself. My days were filled with work or sightseeing. I spent countless hours evaluating my journey through the book writing process. I delved deep into the memories of the past couple of years and spent very little time connecting with anyone at home, including Mark. The few times we would find to connect by phone, the distance between us was evident. He had made the decision to actively pursue relationships with people in the recovery community. He seemed more focused on building those connections than involving me in this part of his journey.

And I had a single-minded focus on my healing. The distance between us felt as vast as the miles between the US and the UK. We were growing apart and neither one of us knew how to reconnect with the other. The events of the last few years had impacted us so differently. And the differences in our ways of coping had caused a distance I could never have seen coming.

I was consumed with my own process of healing. Removing myself from my life at home gave me the space I needed to focus on me and recognize the ways that God was showing up and allowing me to shine my light as a healer and mentor. I became profoundly aware that joy was possible after the pain. Everyone talks about the light at the end of the tunnel, but I was finally seeing it.

LIFE LESSON: When you do things that expand you, that truly take a leap of faith, God/higher power will show up and show off, as long as you are open to magic.

QUESTION: How has God/higher power shown up and showed off for you? Are you open to magic?

26

RETURNING HOME

A s I prepared to return home from my second UK trip, I was both excited for and nervous about the future. For the first time, I was truly focusing on me and how I want to show up in the world. How could I make my little corner of world a better place? It was evident that I was not returning as the same person; this version of me wasn't recognizable to my family. I was even peppered with questions about whether or not I was moving permanently to the UK.

As I've gone deeper into my healing journey, it's helped me forge deeper connections with my children. Over frequent texts and the occasional phone call, I interacted with them more during the UK trip than I had in a very long time. But regrettably, I felt more disconnected from Mark than ever. I often tell people that the day Dylan crashed his car, it was like he put the whole family in the car with him, and we all came out with different injuries and separate time lines for healing.

Nearly losing a child had a massive impact on my

marriage to Mark. The long runs out on country roads, the times spent in worship at church, the date nights, the laughter—they all took a back burner for so long. It's like we forgot about each other; we were in a desperate fight to save ourselves. I've never had a connection with anyone like I've had with Mark. But the quiet man who I fell so deeply in love with became even quieter, lost in the pain of watching his child battle similar demons to his own. I knew how deep this time in our lives impacted me, but it was hard to wrap my head around how it uniquely impacted Mark.

While I was in the UK, building a business, writing a book, and making memories, Mark found comfort in local Narcotics Anonymous meetings. The man who once spent all his time at home with his family was now gone five to seven nights a week. I truly wanted to be supportive of his need to build a support system and new friendships. What I wasn't expecting was the pull he felt toward one of the other meeting attendees. Soon after he started regularly attending, he began making outside plans to socialize with the group, including one particular woman and her children.

Our worlds were growing farther and farther apart.

As much as I wished to swoop in and save Mark like I wanted to save Dylan, I knew that it's not up to me alone. And so I continued to put on my own oxygen mask first and hope and pray that Mark would find his. For the prior year, Dylan was living in Florida. And after multiple stints in rehab, he had finally managed to maintain sobriety for nine months. He still had some physical symptoms with his heart and carotid artery, but long-term sobriety offered him the possibility to get the medical attention he needed.

I saw my son find his own sense of purpose by working

in the addictions community and helping others with similar struggles. I came to the deep acceptance that he wouldn't be returning to Maryland. He needed to find a life in a new location and build his foundation there. And though I missed him terribly, my greatest desire for all my children remained for them to find purpose in this life and to truly be able to show up as they were meant to. When I headed home from the UK, I had no idea what the future held for any of us. I had to trust fall again, trust that God was going to continue to show up and show off as he had done so many times before.

The uncertainty of what was to come was both terrifying and exhilarating because my life looked nothing like what I anticipated even one year earlier. Initially, when I took the trip to the UK, I believed that I was there to learn more about Sidra's teaching, to continue her work and mission. But after spending time abroad, I became aware that there was an even greater reason for me to make this trip. I was learning to find my power, to stand in my truth. I was building my skills as a leader.

It's so hard to see certain seasons of our lives come to a close and to feel the grief and the pain of saying goodbye to those things that are now distant memories. But there's always a new season. Nothing is by chance, as I've come to learn through this whole experience. A friend asked if I wanted to come spend a week in her Florida home. A bit of sunshine felt like exactly the cure I needed to gain some more clarity on my journey.

Divinely, her condo was located only five minutes from the place Dylan now called home.

I'd spent the past year physically and emotionally distanced from Dylan, recognizing that I couldn't save him. For three years of my life I'd completely lost myself in my child's pain. Upon realizing how unhealthy the situation was, I gave Dylan the space to face his pain, and for the first time he was experiencing longer-term sobriety. We made plans to meet for dinner.

I had no idea our dinner conversation that night would bring forth tremendous clarity.

At first, seeing him again was awkward and a little uncomfortable for both of us. Dylan and I talked about his time in Florida, and the foundational building blocks he had begun to place for an independent life as a young adult. I shared with him some of the pain that was still happening in our home, and how I was finding it so hard to understand the disease of addiction.

"Mom," he said, "let me explain something to you. I was born with a God-sized hole in my chest. I tried to fill it with alcohol and drugs. I tried to fill it with gambling and steroids. Everything I tried to fill it with would come up feeling empty. It wasn't until I started to fill that God-sized hole in my chest with the only thing that could fill it, God, that I started to experience some relief from the pain that I have felt since I was a little boy.

"Dad, too, has a God-sized hole in his chest. He's been trying for decades to fill it with anything he can, always coming up short and continuing to feel the pain. He has to learn how to fill that God-sized hole in his chest, exactly as I did. Mom, it's not up to you. Dad needs to figure this out himself."

Because our conversation focused on addiction and the pain that Dylan and Mark had in common, at first I didn't think about how this God-sized hole is in all of us.

And then it profoundly touched me.

My God-sized hole started as a young child, with my father and our toxic relationship that would swing like a pendulum between loving and hurtful. I was constantly trying to fill that vacuum with men who I thought could save me. I continued to repeat circumstances that weren't healthy for myself, and especially for my children. My history of self-harm and self-sabotage—through each experience I would repeat the pain over and over again.

The day that Dylan crashed his car into a tree, the day that changed our whole family, I became single-mindedly focused on filling my own God-sized hole with the only thing that has felt aligned with me. And that's God. It's not up to us to complete anyone else. As much as I wanted to take the lessons that I learned and pour them into others, wishing them to see the bigger picture, it's not up to me. No one could save me from myself, and I can't save another. For the very first time, I was making decisions on how I show up in the world in an effort to gain clarity on the journey that I've taken, to apply the lessons, and to find the purpose in all the pain.

I was no longer running from the pain and the experiences. Instead, I vowed to take a closer look at each one of those experiences, from the very early stages of childhood to now, to find the deeper meaning, to fill the God-sized hole in a way that I have never tried before. I would no longer look for a quick fix or for someone to swoop in and save me. I became determined to save myself, and to hopefully set an example for my children, that they, too, can find a way to fill that God-sized hole and show up in the world exactly as they were meant to.

LIFE LESSON: We have a responsibility to ourselves first, regardless of what is happening around us. Sometimes we need to change our environment to give us perspective to heal.

QUESTION: Is your environment conducive to healing? What would need to change in order to create a healing environment?

27

IT'S OVER

It turns out my story was far from over.

I returned home from the UK filled with anxiety, completely unsure of what was next. I was excited about the fact that I had finished a first draft of my book, that I had completed a daunting process, but little did I know I still needed to write the final chapters. On the plane back, I reflected on some of the pivotal moments that had happened in the previous months, including reaching out to Will, Eastyn's dad, to ask if he would be willing to have lunch with me. We met at a restaurant and I talked about the challenges that I was facing in my marriage.

I was transparent with Will about the healing business that I had been cultivating and how my personal life was falling apart. Though he knew I was traveling, he had very little knowledge of the changes in me since Dylan's crash. Because of the disconnect with my family, my parents, and my sisters, it left me very few options for how to navigate potentially leaving my marriage. Will, without hesitation, said that he would always have his door open for me if I needed a place to stay.

I reflected on sharing a chapter from the book with Mark earlier. It was a sacred chapter, the one of the vision of Dylan coming into our room. I played its original audio recording for him, hoping that he would have the same strong response as others who had heard it.

I had no idea that his response was going to be flat and unemotional. His comments were "I don't know how you remember all this" and "You talk too slow."

I remembered a few days before leaving the UK, reviewing the chapter of the fairy tale and thinking that if I got Mark on the phone, maybe I could get him to see the beauty of what we had and that maybe we could get that back. I reached out to him, and he was unavailable for a full twenty-four hours. I desperately wanted to share with him where we once were, in the hopes of getting us back there, but when I finally got him on the phone, I had the profound realization that living in a toxic environment with him was killing my spirit.

I told him there was no way that I could continue on the way that we were without losing myself. When I landed in the US, Mark was at the airport waiting for me. We talked the entire way home, which was very different than the relationship that we had for the last several months. We were sharing different things about what was happening in each of our lives, but it was very apparent that we were in two totally separate worlds, having our own unique experiences. On that ride home, I shared the news that I had finished the book, hoping that he would see the importance of the UK trips I had taken and the work that I was doing, but he didn't seem connected to what I was sharing at all.

He was in his world, existing and trying to heal, and I

was in mine. And for some reason, those two worlds were completely separate from each other. Walking in the door of my home that evening, nothing felt the same. I knew something significant in me had changed, and I felt like I no longer belonged in that space. I was exhausted from travel and climbed into the bed that we shared, neither one of us touching the other one and falling asleep quickly. I had no idea that would be the last night that I would spend in our home.

When I woke up the next morning, I noticed that Mark wasn't wearing his wedding ring. I was shocked, because in all the years that we had been married, I had never seen that ring leave his finger. I asked if he was done, and he said yes without hesitation. We calmly tried to discuss a plan to coexist in the house. My hope was that I would buy more time for myself to establish this new career of Soul Center before moving out on my own, maybe giving me some time to figure out next steps.

He suggested that I move into the basement, the same space where I would work and see clients. I didn't even process the conversation. I just started trying to work out the physical move to the basement, which would require me to get a bed and new sheets. As that conversation closed, I felt numb. So much had happened in such a short time. I was jet-lagged, unrested, and anxious. I drove to Target and walked through the bedding section aimlessly. The weight of the decisions facing me was starting to set in, and I had no idea how I was going to do this.

I made my way back to the car and sat in the parking lot. I pleaded with God, *What do You want me to do? I don't know how to handle this. I don't know how I'm going to live in this very basement where so much of my pain has happened—receiving news of the car crash, desperately searching for rehab centers, and answering calls from the doctors which would interrupt my workday and my sacred space. I need a sign.* I drove home in silence.

Will's car was waiting at the end of my driveway, waiting to pick Eastyn up from the bus.

I got out of my car and walked up to Will's driver's side window. I asked him if he was serious about his offer to allow me to move back into his home, the very same home I had previously lived in, a place that held so many memories of when Will and I were married. So many decisions were made in that space. He said he wouldn't have offered if he wasn't serious.

He just needed a little bit of time to make arrangements for me and get the space organized in order for me to be able to move in. And so I decided to pack a bag and proceeded to spend multiple nights at various friends' houses, couch surfing, trying to work out what was best for me and for Eastyn. I told Mark there was no way that I could continue to stay in the house with him and coexist. I told him that Will had offered to allow me to move in, imagining that he would have a huge problem with me moving in with my ex-husband, and yet, without hesitation, he agreed it was the best thing for me to do.

At the time, I didn't realize in moving out, I was also surrendering my career as a hairdresser, because I would no longer have access to my working space. I was in survival mode, making the decisions as quickly as I needed to, to try to save myself.

Abruptly stopping my business had a massive impact on my clients. People who I had spent years pouring into and serving in the community were now gone from my life, many of them having no idea what I was facing in my personal life. I didn't feel I had time to explain what was happening, and reaching out to people and sharing the pain that I was going through, and recounting the experience of the last couple of weeks, was something I couldn't bring myself to do. All my energy was going into surviving. I had spent years cultivating relationships with my clients at the expense of spending time with my family. I spent countless, long days behind the chair, sacrificing my evenings, and weekends, and holidays to make sure that my clients always felt cared for and loved, and now I had to focus on myself.

Will's basement level was a space that would be perfect for me. I would have access to an office space, a bedroom, a bathroom, everything that I needed, and we would just need to share a kitchen. I became focused on creating a space for myself, where I could start the journey to healing independently. I had no idea how I was going to move an entire house's worth of stuff into a new space, yet God continued to show off by sending me people who were available to help me pack boxes and move the most essential belongings into my new living space. I believed it was going to take weeks for me to go through an entire house's worth of stuff, packing up and purging, but because of the help I was provided with, I was able to move in one weekend.

Despite Will's selfless offer to host, it soon became very clear that he was totally overwhelmed with the upheaval of a life that he had created in routine and structure for just him and Eastyn. I felt a tremendous amount of guilt as I watched him continue to move my things into his space, sacrificing and putting aside his own feelings to support me, his ex-wife. There were so many details to work through each day between packing, and purging, and moving, and reestablishing a life, that it left me very little time to process what was happening. I would get in bed at night in my new space, in my new bedroom alone, and I would find my mind racing with grief, anxiety, and fear.

I would find myself sleeping with the lights on, and when I would finally fall asleep, it would be for a short period of time before I would wake up gasping for air, feeling like I was suffocating. The magnitude of yet another trauma would play out every single night for weeks, and I would get up again every day, focused on trying to reset my life and create a safe space for myself. Also, in leaving my home, I left my closet, the sacred haven where I had done so much healing and helped other people on their journey to healing. I became fiercely determined to create another physical space with the same healing properties, where I could continue to grow and thrive. I was trying to establish a new life and trying to create a healing space for others at the same time.

It was overwhelming.

I had been using marijuana to numb the pain of my circumstances. But once I removed myself from the home with Mark, I realized how much I was relying on a substance to avoid facing the dark parts of myself, the parts that still needed to heal. I knew I didn't want to spend my life numbing my pain and avoiding things that I needed to face in order to heal. I wanted to live life awakened and with purpose. Plus, with all this change happening in my personal life, I was planning the first ever Soul Center live in-person event.

The Soul Center team was made up of two friends from the UK who I met on Clubhouse and two friends from the US. We had been consistently connecting on Clubhouse, hosting rooms for people and building our following. In addition, we met once a week via Zoom for connection and planning sessions. Though Nimesh had helped me cultivate the mission and vision for Soul Center, he remained on the outskirts of the original team dynamic. Unfortunately, he was unable to make it to our first live event.

People were flying in from various parts of the country, including members of the Soul Center team, flying in from the UK. Because they were visiting the US for the first time, we weren't just planning the event; we were planning things for us to do, to entertain them, and give them the experience of being in the States. It was chaotic, stressful, and exciting, all at the same time.

The event was fire. As I stood in a room filled with people, inspiring them to awaken into their soul's purpose, I knew that I was meant to be seen and heard as a healer, as a mentor. I felt completely aligned with my purpose, and the attendees of the event wanted to stay in the room well after the event had closed for the day, so that they could continue to soak in the powerful, spiritual experience.

Though the event was incredible and life-changing, it regrettably became apparent that there was a disconnect with the members of the Soul Center team. The team was formed out of friendship and connection. But there were many times while I was struggling with my life circumstances, that made it hard to show up as a leader. Though I was in survival mode personally and felt stretched thin, I was also aware I was being called for more. This, along with a deep disconnect in our core values, made for miscommunication and frustration.

I had to put myself first, make my healing a priority, and establish a new normal. It became very clear that I was showing up, but others around me could not recognize this new version of me who was fighting to create a new life and close out a chapter. Looking back, I believe it was very hard for some of the members of the team to comprehend the magnitude of what was happening in my personal life. I never felt more aligned with who I am and how I'm showing up in the world than I did during that event, and yet, some of the team felt that I wasn't being authentic. They felt that if I was showing people this empowered version of me *and* struggling with my personal life, that somehow those two things didn't connect . . . even if it was the furthest thing from the truth.

I was finally in an environment that supported me and the changes I was making. The team gathered for a debrief a couple of weeks after the event, and the tension on the call was palpable. I felt like I was sitting on a call with strangers, all of us coming into the mix with our different opinions and perceptions of what was happening. There was criticism of me and what I was going through and how I was handling it. Ultimately, it led to the decision for the Soul Center team to go our separate ways. I was completely focused on saving myself, knowing that there was no way that I could convince others that what I was doing was the right thing.

I'd spent so much time on Clubhouse in Soul Center. And every time I would announce the club, I would say, "It's our club," referencing the team. But I would always be corrected by one of the team, saying, "No, Stacey, it's *your* club." It took me losing an entire team to recognize Soul Center is, in fact, mine. You see, healers need healing too. If anyone tells you that they're healed, they're probably not being honest with you, because as long as we're still walking this earth, we are healing.

As I began to feel a little safer and settled in my new environment, I experienced a deeper acceptance of who I am, and I made the conscious decision to surrender using marijuana. I wanted to feel all the emotions, even the pain, and process the experience of going through another divorce and my effort to be a healthier, happier, more stable version of myself.

My contact with Mark remained extremely limited. Our interactions were based around the logistical choices necessary during the divorce process. He reached out to me and said it was time for us to sell the dream home where we had created so many memories, and also experienced so much pain. The housing market was at its peak, and it was the beginning of summer, a time when so many families make the decision to move.

I realized yet again, I would have to go back to the house to pack up the rest of my life and face more of the grief of ending a life chapter that I thought was my happy ending. I had spent so much time and money building a home, establishing a safe haven for my kids to come and be with us, a space where we experienced family dinners, holidays, and now all those memories were being left behind. All I had were a few boxes, a few pieces of furniture, and the ending of my fairy tale.

I was blessed with a really incredible support system through this time. It's not the number of people you have around you, but the quality. As I was trying to recover from all the heartbreak, Nimesh suggested that we take an adventure to Mexico.

I probably wasn't in the right headspace for a vacation, and yet, changing my orbit sounded appealing. We went to a beautiful resort, enjoying the sunshine and the water. I was detoxing from everything, releasing the things that no longer served me. I grieved at the end of the fairy tale. I allowed my body to be cleansed of the marijuana that I had relied on for so long, and I began to radically accept myself and the reality that I was going into a new season of my life, independent and free.

When I arrived home from nine relaxing days in a tropical location, I was met with more chaos. Will had worked so hard to create a calm life for him and Eastyn, and it felt like the chaos was mine, that there were things that were happening that were unavoidable. We had a water leak that flooded my new living space, and shortly thereafter, we were hit with an unexpected tornado that damaged the yard and our home. Logical or not, I felt responsible for the chaos wrapping Will's former quiet life. And yet, through all this chaos, I was determined to create a safe haven to allow me to thrive and to do the work I'm meant to do.

I realized that people who didn't understand my journey were falling away, and the people that did were giving me the space and the support that I needed to heal. My circle had never been smaller than it is was then, and yet, I had never felt more supported on my journey. I knew that the people who were surrounding me were the ones who truly saw who I am and believe in my ability to help others and to shine.

THE MORE I have accepted who I am in all the ways, the more I thrive, and the more I attract people who see me for who I am. There are decades of programming that I am finally releasing. I am stepping into my power.

I'm working hard on creating a self-care routine. I recognize the importance of all the training that I have done throughout my life, and that when I apply the skills that I teach people every day and I shed what's not serving me, I'm able to show up in the world the way that I'm meant to, the way that I deserve to. There are so many practical parts of divorce that I hadn't even thought about until they were staring me in the face. Over the years with Mark, we had each taken on different responsibilities in our day-to-day life, and now I am faced with taking on all those responsibilities myself—the monthly bills, car payment, car insurance, cell phone. Much of my days are consumed with getting these practical parts figured out, recognizing that I am navigating life independently now. It took me to the age of forty-five to realize that no other person is going to complete me.

I realize now that I have to feel whole and complete as me, allowing myself to flourish and navigate through the fear of doing this by myself. I'm sure there are many people who could be critical of the fact that I have moved back in with my daughter's father. It seems like a strange decision to make, to go from one living situation to the next. Relying on a man is probably what people would assume, but my little girl nearly lost her brother at the age of five, and when that happened, I feel like she lost her mother for several years too. Now, at the age of nine, she has faced more in her young life than many kids her age.

Being in this space with Will has given me the blessing of being able to show up as a mother in a way that I would not have been able to if I lived somewhere else. We've been navigating a beautiful co-parenting relationship and providing our little girl the support she needs during another significant transition in her life. I have been able to be present for her in exactly the way that I want to, spending quality time with her, connecting with her, mothering her. Eastyn knows that this arrangement is temporary, and though she enjoys having both of her parents under one roof, she talks about her excitement when I do move to my own space and how she'll have a new bedroom and time with her mom independently. People may judge my decision for moving in with Will, but I have no regrets.

This was the right thing for all of us and has allowed me the blessing of seeing Will in a new light. He has supported me when so many have walked away, and he made sure that I was given a safe space to heal. This space has created an environment where I am able to thrive. I'm finally sleeping through the night. I'm not waking up, gasping for air. And I'm able to do the work that I love.

Everyone chooses to handle trauma differently. I've definitely been through a lot of trauma in my life, and in the past, when my life has been upended, the old Stacey would blow shit up. Meaning, I would take a chaotic situation and make it even more challenging. But this version of me, the version that is committed to healing, is aware that I can't just blow shit up. I'm aware that I need to create space for me to process things, to be able to face those dark parts of myself; so, recently, I planned a weekend away for myself, time to rest and rejuvenate. And at the last minute, my plans fell through. I decided, on a Friday night, to go out and release some of the stress that I had been feeling, only to find myself in a situation that not only didn't align with who I am, but became unsafe. In the past, that situation would've started a snowball effect, but this new version of me took control, recognizing that sometimes we stumble, but now, I have to make the choice to get up and respond differently. I have to be true to this version of myself, and even if I stumble, I must get back up and keep going. My life depends on it.

When I think back to the time I felt most aligned in all four bodies—physical, mental, emotional, and spiritual—it was at the age of forty. I was in the best shape of my life. I was deeply connected spiritually, and the decisions that I made every day helped me to feel aligned and intentional. I realize now that I was in training, that learning all those habits was preparing me for the challenges ahead, and that I was already given the techniques that would pull me out of the darkness I was currently facing. I've become fiercely dedicated to using those very same techniques now, not only to help me continue going every day, but to help me thrive and shine in the way that I'm meant to.

I have no idea what's next. I don't know where I'll be living, when I'll move out, what kind of space I'll be living in, but I am so excited for what's coming. I've created an environment that feels loving, and safe, and protected. My business as a healer and a mentor is thriving. When I chose to surrender the old life and radically accept this new life, everything started to shift, and I'm having a profound impact on the people that I'm working with, and I'm watching their lives change as well.

I'm working with clients from all around the world, helping people navigate through seasons in their life where things are changing and imparting the wisdom that I've learned from so many years of heartache and pain. I am showing up, and the universe is absolutely showing off. I'm shining my light and authentically being me while encouraging others to do the same.

I didn't write this book for me, though the process has been very therapeutic. It's also been extremely painful. When we go through deep seasons of trauma and pain, it's hard enough to survive it, let alone to relive it, but I keep an image in my head, and I think about it every day. I imagine a woman going through upheaval in her life, unsure of what's next and how to navigate through it. I picture her walking into her local bookstore and aimlessly wandering down the rows of books, searching through different sections of the bookstore, longing for answers that will help her move forward. I picture her placing her finger along the shelf, dragging her hand along the rows of the books, and her hand stops right in front of mine.

She picks up my book and holds it in her hands, and finds some answers and some inspiration to move through this painful season in her life. I hold this image in my head as I navigate through sharing these stories, this journey, this transformation and this healing, and I hold it close because she is the one that I went through this painful process for. My greatest hope is that this book will change the life of that woman, because even if it helps one soul, it was worth it.

LIFE LESSON: When you are going through a rebirth, every aspect of your life can be turned inside out. But in many ways this is what's needed. The more you resist, the harder it becomes. Always remember that there is light at the end of the tunnel, but sometimes it feels like a long tunnel.

QUESTION: Does your life look like you expected it to? Have you experienced a rebirth?

28

NEW SEASON

If you could imagine the pain of the last several years in my life, like wounds appearing on my body, some of those wounds have begun to heal, even forming a nice scar that's no longer tender to the touch, but some of the wounds are still open and revisiting these more recent events in my life feels a little bit like pouring salt in them. I've spent over two decades of my life loving Mark. Whether we were co-parenting or we were married, we were always connected. And for the last several months, the only exchange we shared is a random text about things involving our divorce.

I've learned recently that he's seriously seeing someone that he met in the program. As much as I know we're not meant to be together in this season, I'm still grieving. I'm grieving the loss of us traveling, experiencing grandchildren, retiring, and growing old together. I'm also learning to get really comfortable with being on my own, making my own schedule, and living life on my terms without considering another.

I spent years working with clients behind the chair every day. I gave up nights and weekends in order to make the money I needed and to accommodate my clients. I loved what I did as a hairdresser for so long, and yet I knew that God was calling me to more. In this new season, I work remotely with clients from around the world. I have the beautiful blessing of waking up every morning and getting my little girl ready for school and waving to her as she gets on and off the bus each day. Aydan is following in my foot-steps and pursuing a career in cosmetology. My days are filled with healing services, readings, and mentorship.

One client who I worked with recently said, "Through this awakening, I am realizing I am not changing who I am, but discarding who I am not." I've had the blessing of culti-vating a vision for a new and better Soul Center with Nimesh. We've been implementing that vision not only in our Clubhouse rooms, but in our channeled mentorship program and the joint Akashic readings that we do for people. Nimesh had a vision of using his voice through a podcast, and he recently invited me to join in a series of episodes wherein we share stories of our personal journeys in an effort to help open people to a greater way of being. It soon became apparent that the dynamic we fostered in Clubhouse moderating rooms together effortlessly carried over into the platform of podcasting.

I continue to be in awe of how clients are divinely guided to us. One client was out hiking solo in Sedona when she stumbled upon Nimesh and me in the *Spiritual Journey* podcast. She listened intently, and then decided to reach out and embark on a three-month journey with us in the mentorship program that we work on together. My mind was blown at the way God has taken my passion for helping people and allowed me the gift of helping others, not only in my local community, but globally. I was watching our early hopes and vision become something truly impactful.

As I spent more time on my own in this new season, I also became aware of how much I neglected my physical body during the times of survival mode. I wanted to feel the runner's high again, to challenge myself to get back in shape.

Three and a half months ago, I laced up my running shoes again, got on the treadmill in the very basement where I started my journey nine years earlier. I put on my headphones and allowed myself to jog until winded. Three months later, I was seeing the shift in my body that I've missed so much. I've created more space for the rhythmic, calming, meditative state of running to be a part of my life. I'm feeling its impact on my mental health, as I make my own needs a priority. I'm getting to know this new me, and she is awesome.

I am unsure of all the details of the next season, but I am so excited for the changes that I see happening. My greatest desire has been to walk through this season of healing, to become more aware of who I am, and loving that person. And I recognize that the more that I love myself, the more I attract love to me. As Nimesh and I continue to build a vision for the future, I look forward to many, many more clients that we can inspire to make the same changes that I'm committed to every day for myself.

AFTERWORD

In my early teens, I was diagnosed with attention deficit disorder, or ADD. I wonder now if I was actually channeling messages and that's what was causing the fireworks to go off in my brain. But either way, I found it challenging to sit down and write my story.

I tried unsuccessfully to work with a writing coach, sitting before my computer and tapping out the words, only to look back on the writing and feel frustrated that it wasn't conveying the story in the way that I wanted. My friend Nimesh suggested that we try recording the book on audio and then have it transcribed. It was a unique approach to the process of writing a book, but one that felt a little more natural. I know that there is power in using my voice, so we proceeded to make an initial document of bullet points, a chronological list of the events that happened throughout my years. I had practice in telling some of the story through the various Clubhouse rooms.

Emotionally, it's easier to capture one event in a brief story for a couple of minutes on a Clubhouse stage. I'm able to go to the place of darkness, share that small piece of the story, and then release it. But the process of sitting down and going through the pain of each event, regularly, telling it in detail, took me to a very different emotional place.

The process of writing a book, I believe, is very similar to the process of preparing to run a marathon. When we hear that someone is running a marathon, we only picture them completing its 26.2 miles. We fail to recognize the countless hours and days that are spent training in preparation. There were many days when running felt like the last thing I wanted to do. Sometimes the weather conditions were awful and I'd be out running with soggy shoes in the rain. Other days, I would find it hard to complete the same sort of stride, to get the distance in. It felt like I had lead in my shoes. But I never gave up; I continued to show up every day, no matter how hard the challenges were, because I had a goal.

I'm reliving my story, trying to recount all the details for the listener. There are days where I've sat before this very microphone, trying to find the words to express the emotions, the pain, and find the delivered lessons in it.

Not only am I reliving the story of Dylan, the magical moments when God showed up for our family, but I've also had to process things that I didn't even know I had acknowledged before now. And here I am, processing all my pain, my story, and doing it publicly, open for the world to see, to scrutinize, and possibly to judge.

There are mixed emotions. Some are fear-based and others are inspiring. I have been so desperate to create a new legacy for my children. The theme of my life for too many decades was shame and guilt. Now I have found a new determination to show my kids the power of healing, of showing up as you were divinely created, to live out your purpose.

I recently reached out to my older children. They knew that I was in the process of writing a book, but now it was time to share it with them. I wonder if I am doing them the service that I hope I am, by changing the legacy of our family. But I am also profoundly aware that by putting our story on display, I could cause them more pain. I don't know how they're going to feel to learn so many intimate details of our family and my journey. I wonder about the controversy that I may stir, recounting my experiences of growing up in the Mormon faith. Was it the way that my father interpreted the religion? Or is it the religion? I'm still not sure, but my experiences are my own and they needed to be shared. Writing this book is more than a desire; it's a calling.

The only thing I know for sure is that this story is my own, and that maybe, hopefully, it will help someone.

That by finding and reading my story, something in them stirs.

My hope is that maybe by me being open, authentic, and vulnerable, it will create space for others to do the same.

My prayer, as I move forward into this next season, is that this book will inspire you, my dear reader, to find the deeper meaning in *your* journey. To really get honest with yourself and to embrace the inspiration to show up in the world, as you were divinely created.

ACKNOWLEDGMENTS

This book happened because of the people below:

Katelynn—for your unwavering love of your family no matter what it looks like. For cheering me on and supporting my vision. For fighting fiercely for all of us. I love you.

Dylan—for allowing me to honor my perspective of our story. For recovery in all forms. I love you.

Aydan—for honoring your own unique journey and being braver than I'll ever be. I love you.

Eastyn—for giving me a reason to wake up every morning and always being open to more kisses and hugs. I love you.

Patty—my sister, mother figure, and very dear friend. I became a hairdresser because of you. Thank you for your unwavering love and support. You are the family I always needed.

Jessi—from scalp massages to crying with me to road-trip buddies and photo shoots, life is better with you in it. Tattoo slap.

Nims—buddy, you met me in my most vulnerable state and chose to join the roller coaster. Without you, getting this book done would have been nearly impossible. Thank you for holding space, embracing my mess, and encouraging me to be me. You and Merlin hold a magical place in the journey of this book. I am forever grateful. Thank you for teaching me the power of the word "sure."

Will—we have embarked on a beautiful co-parenting relationship. Thank you for giving me a place to land while I healed. Thank you for showing me the power of forgiveness and compassion.

Patrick—thank you for taking on this project and for giving it all you've got. Meeting you was a blessing. I look forward to more books ahead. (Wait, did I just say that?!)

Krista—thank you for taking the vision I had on my heart for this cover and making my dream a reality. I feel blessed to have you on this project.

To our local community—thank you for showing up for our family in our darkest hour. Not one need went unmet. You have shown me the beauty of small-town living, and for that I am grateful. I vow to continue paying it forward.

To my clients (both healing and hair)—thank you for years of love and support. You all have become family. I am blessed.

To the Soul Center community on Clubhouse—you have become my family and a place for me to learn and grow more than I ever could have imagined. Thank you for being a part of my vision. May this community continue to grow and inspire others on their own journey to healing.

ABOUT THE AUTHOR

Stacey Brown has had empathic intuitive abilities her entire life. After a family trauma, she left her successful career as a hairdresser to dedicate her life to helping people on their journey to healing. She does this through intuitive readings, spiritual mentorship and coaching, and her successful podcast *Spiritual Journey: Path to Awakening* with Nimesh Radia. Stacey is the founder of Soul Center, a global community inspiring individuals to awaken to their soul's purpose. She lives in Maryland with her youngest daughter.

stacey-brown.com

 instagram.com/staceybrown_555

Printed in Great Britain
by Amazon

36506042R00118